D1859835

THE ORIGIN OF LETTERS AND NUMERALS

THE ORIGIN OF LETTERS AND NUMERALS

ACCORDING TO THE SEFER YETZIRAH

BY

PHINEAS MORDELL

KALPAZ

©Reserved
All rights reserved. No part of this work may be reproduced, stored, adapted, or transmitted in any form or by any means, electronic, mechanical, photocopying, micro-filming recording or otherwise, or translated in any language, without the prior written permission of the copyright owner and the publisher. The book is sold subject to the condition that it shall not, by way of trade or otherwise, be lent, resold, hired out, or otherwise circulated without the prior publisher's written consent in any form of binding or cover other than that in which it is published.

The views and opinions expressed in this book are author(s) own and the facts reported by them have been verified to the extent possible, and the publishers are not in any way liable for the same.

ISBN: 978-93-5128-947-0(HB)

First Published in 1914
Indian Reprint in 2017

Published by

Kalpaz Publications
C-30, Satyawati Nagar,
Delhi – 110052
E-mail: kalpaz@hotmail.com
Website: kalpazpublications.com
Ph.: +91-9212142040

CHAP. I

THE ORIGIN OF LETTERS AND NUMERALS ACCORDING TO THE SEFER YETZIRAH

BY PHINEAS MORDELL

THERE is hardly another book in Jewish literature, the Bible and the Talmud excepted, that has been so much commented upon as the Sefer Yetzirah. It has been the subject of deep study, not only to the mystic, who regarded it as the source of esoteric lore, but also to the philosopher and the Talmudist. And yet, despite all the efforts of a large number of scholars of repute for more than a thousand years, the Sefer Yetzirah remains a sealed book. The various commentaries upon it are more apt to bewilder the student than to enlighten him. Indeed, it would seem that every commentator endeavored to read his own views and theories into this little book, with hardly any concern whether they agreed with the text or not.

There is no book in Jewish literature that is so difficult to understand as the Sefer Yetzirah. For it was originally written in an obscure half-mystical style. To make matters worse, the commentators of the eighth or of the ninth century blended the original "Sefer Yetzirah" with an early commentary, which may be referred to as "Sefer Yetzirah II." It thus happened that all the commentaries written on the "Sefer Yetzirah" since the beginning of the tenth century are chiefly based on this commentary and not on the original Sefer Yetzirah. Although the Sefer Yetzirah is exceedingly hard to understand, the solution of its many difficulties is not impossible. The reason why they have remained so long an unsolved problem is partly due to a lack of knowledge of Hebrew orthography, on which the Sefer Yetzirah is based. In spite of the numerous works written on Hebrew orthography since the beginning of the tenth century, there is not one which may be considered as really based on the Hebrew. For the Hebrew orthography which has been and is still taught, is not Hebrew but Arabic. The Hebrew grammarians under Arabic influence came to believe that those rules of orthography which the Arab grammarians invented for the language of the Koran hold good also for the language of the Old Testament. When the Honorable Mayer Sulzberger heard me expressing my views on Hebrew orthography, he advised me to make a study of the Sefer Yetzirah which in his opinion constitutes the earliest Hebrew grammar extant. Finding that my views on Hebrew orthography harmonized with those of the Sefer Yetzirah, I made an exhaustive study of it. After many years of study, I reached the conclusion that the Sefer Yetzirah, as the earliest Hebrew grammar, contains not only the fundamental rules of Hebrew orthography, but also an account of the origin of letters and numerals. This account it is my present purpose to seth forth[1]).

[1]) I wish to express here my thanks to J. Broyde, Miss Henrietta Szold, Prof. Henry Malter, and Dr Isaac Husik for many courtesies extended to me in this work, both in the arrangement of the material and in style.

The first Mishnah reads as follows: שלשים ושתים נתיבות פליאות הקק יה יהוה צבאות בסופר וספור וספר.

"Thirty-two mysterious ways has the Lord, the Lord of hosts, ordained through Scribe, Script and Scroll."

The thirty-two mysterious ways are the twenty-two letters of the Hebrew alphabet, which represent thirty-two sounds.[2])

In accordance with the belief of the ancients that the letters are of divine origin, the Sefer Yetzirah explains that the thirty-two ways of wisdom were ordained by God through:

(1) סופר (Scribe), the man whom God inspired to invent the alphabet;

(2) ספור (Script), the letters;

(3) ספר (Scroll), the material on which the letters were displayed.

In order to show how the twenty-two letters of the alphabet constitute the thirty-two ways of wisdom, the author proceeds to the division of the letters in the second and following Mishnahs. He divides them into simple and double sounds, and also into vowels and consonants. The simple letters he called פשוטות, and the double, כפולות; the vowels, אמות (=אבות), and the consonants, תולדות. Altogether they form thirty-two sounds: the twenty sounds of the ten[3]) double letters, and the twelve of the twelve simple letters.

[2]) All the commentators explain that the thirty-two ways of wisdom are the twenty-two letters and the ten Sefirot. Below will be found the reasons why the present writer cannot accept this interpretation.

[3]) Below will be explained that, according to the Sefer Yetzirah, there are ten double letters and not only seven, as is believed by all commentators since Saadya.

The Sefer Yetzirah[4]) emphasizes that the number of the double letters is no less and no more than ten, and the number of the simple letters no less and no more than twelve. The Sefer Yetzirah urges us to investigate and examine the letters, that we may have a clear insight into the subject. This proves that, at the time when the book was written, the nature of the letters, or of some of them, was misunderstood. We know, indeed, that at the time when the Greek translation of the Bible was made, it was believed that the ע, for example, could be transliterated by *e*, *a*, or *g*, and the translators accordingly rendered it variously by one of these three sounds.

Arguments have repeatedly been advanced in favor of the view that the Hebrew ע had not only the sound of the Arabic ع, but also of the غ. But according to the Sefer Yetzirah, the ע is a simple letter. If it has the sound of ع it is impossible that it should also have the sound of غ. Moreover, if the ע was originally a vowel only and had no sound of *g*, as maintained by Jerome, it can have only one vowel sound. If we ascribe to it the sound of *A*, it is impossible that it should have also the sound of *E* or *O*, etc. Furthermore, according to the Sefer Yetzirah, the letters ח, ט, צ are also simple letters, and each must have had only one sound and not two as in Arabic.

The author of the Sefer Yetzirah apparently cautioned against the very errors and mistakes into which all writers on Hebrew grammar have fallen. By dividing the twenty-two Hebrew letters into ten double and twelve simple, representing thirty-two sounds, the author desired to make clear how different the

[4]) See text, § 3.

Hebrew alphabet is from the alphabet which is known as Arabic and which the Arabs themselves used to call *sūri*. By *sūri* was apparently meant Assyrian. The so-called Arabic alphabet consisted originally of only seventen letters. It was apparently originally invented to represent the Assyrian-Babylonian language, which consisted of seventeen or eighteen sounds. Hence the name "*sūri*." When the Arabs, whose original alphabet was the Himyarite, consisting of twenty-eight letters, adopted the "*sūri*" alphabeth, they gave to some "*sūri*" letters two or even three sounds, and such letters are each counted now as two or three letters.

As according to the Sefer Yetzirah the Hebrew alphabet consists of ten double letters and twelve simple, therefore to each double letter must be ascribed two sounds and to each simple letter only one sound without any regard to their value in Arabic.

The best transliteration of the double letters is as follows: אַ = *e*, אָ = *o*, בּ = *b*, ב = *v*, גּ = *g*, ג = as English *j* (?) דּ = *d*, ד = *th* in "*the*," וּ = *u*, ו = *w*, כּ = *k*, כ = German *ch* or Arabic *ḫ*, פּ = *p*, פ = *f*, or *ph*, ר = *r*, ר = *r* or Arabic *ġ*, שׁ = *sh*, שׂ = French *j* (?), תּ = *t*, ת = *th* in "*think*."

The best transliteration of the simple letters is as follows: ה = *h*, ז = English *z*, ח = *ḥ* (Arabic *ḥ*, ט = *t*, י = German *i*, ל = *l*, מ = *m*, נ = *n*, ס = *s*, ע = *u*, צ = *tz*, ק = *k*.

After giving this division of the letters, the Sefer Yetzirah shows how, from these twenty-two letters, all the words that have ever existed or ever will exist can be formed.[5])

[5]) See text, §§ 5, 6 and 7.

Biliteral combinations upon which all other combinations are based.

אא	אב	אג	אד	אה	או	אז	אח	אט	אי	אכ	אל	אמ	אנ	אס	אע	אפ	אצ	אק	אר	אש	את
בא	בב	בג	בד	בה	בו	בז	בח	כט	בי	בכ	בל	במ	בנ	בס	בע	בפ	בצ	בק	בר	בש	בת
גא	גב	גג	גד	גה	גו	גז	גח	גט	גי	גכ	גל	גמ	גנ	גס	גע	גפ	גצ	גק	גר	גש	גת
דא	דב	דג	דד	דה	דו	דז	דח	דט	די	דכ	דל	דמ	דנ	דס	דע	דפ	דצ	דק	דר	דש	דת
הא	הב	הג	הד	הה	הו	הז	הח	הט	הי	הכ	הל	המ	הנ	הס	הע	הפ	הצ	הק	הר	הש	הת
וא	וב	וג	וד	וה	וו	וז	וח	וט	וי	וכ	ול	ומ	ונ	וס	וע	ופ	וצ	וק	ור	וש	ות
וא	זב	זג	זד	זה	זו	זז	זח	זט	זי	זכ	זל	זמ	זנ	זס	זע	זפ	זצ	זק	זר	זש	זת
חא	חב	חג	חד	חה	חו	חז	חח	חט	חי	חכ	חל	חמ	חנ	חס	חע	חפ	חצ	חק	חר	חש	חת
טא	טב	טג	טד	טה	טו	טז	טח	טט	טי	טכ	טל	טמ	טנ	טס	טע	טפ	טצ	טק	טר	טש	טת
יא	יב	יג	יד	יה	יו	יז	יח	יט	יי	יכ	יל	ימ	ינ	יס	יע	יפ	יצ	יק	יר	יש	ית
כא	כב	כג	כד	כה	כו	כז	כח	כט	כי	ככ	כל	כמ	כנ	כס	כע	כפ	כצ	כק	כר	כש	כת
לא	לב	לג	לד	לה	לו	לז	לח	לט	לי	לכ	לל	למ	לנ	לס	לע	לפ	לצ	לק	לר	לש	לת
מא	מב	מג	מד	מה	מו	מז	מח	מט	מי	מכ	מל	ממ	מנ	מס	מע	מפ	מצ	מק	מר	מש	מת
נא	נב	נג	נד	נה	נו	נז	נח	נט	ני	נכ	נל	נמ	ננ	נס	נע	נפ	נצ	נק	נר	גש	נת
סא	סב	סג	סד	סה	סו	סז	סח	סט	סי	סכ	סל	סמ	סנ	סס	סע	ספ	סצ	סק	סר	סש	סת
עא	עב	עג	עד	עה	עו	עז	עח	עט	עי	עכ	על	עמ	ענ	עס	עע	עפ	עצ	עק	עד	עש	עת
פא	פב	פג	פד	פה	פו	פז	פח	פט	פי	פכ	פל	פמ	פנ	פס	פע	פפ	פצ	פק	פר	פש	פת
צא	צב	צג	צד	צה	צו	צז	צח	צט	צי	צכ	צל	צמ	צנ	צס	צע	צפ	צצ	צק	צר	צש	צת
קא	קב	קג	קד	קה	קו	קז	קח	קט	קי	קכ	קל	קמ	קנ	קס	קע	קפ	קצ	קק	קר	קש	קת
רא	רב	רג	רד	רה	רו	רז	רח	רט	רי	רכ	רל	רמ	רנ	רס	רע	רפ	רצ	רק	רר	רש	רת
שא	שב	שג	שד	שה	שו	שז	שח	שט	שי	שכ	של	שמ	שנ	שס	שע	שפ	שצ	שק	שר	שש	שת
תא	תב	תג	תד	תה	תו	תז	תח	תט	תי	תכ	תל	תמ	תנ	תס	תע	תפ	תצ	תק	תר	תש	תת

The purpose of the author was to emphasize the superiority of alphabetic writing over the non-alphabetic writing (ideographic and syllabic) used by all the nations of antiquity, and even now by a great portion of mankind. If we arrange alphabetically all biliteral combinations, as the Sefer Yetzirah directs, joining א with all letters, ב with all letters, etc., there must result a list of 484 combinations ($22^2 = 484$). (See preceding page.)

Furthermore, by the expression וחוזר הגלגל פנים ואחור וסימן לדבר עין למעלה ענג ועין למטה נגע the Sefer Yetzirah indicates that the biliteral combinations can be made the basis of all triliteral combinations. If we desire to arrange all the triliteral combinations that can be formed from the 22 letters, their number will be 22^3 or 10,648. For this it would be necessary to draw up twenty-two tables with the biliteral combinations, leaving sufficient space between every two combinations for the addition of a letter. On one table an א would have to be added at the beginning of each biliteral combination, and the result would be a complete table of 484 triliteral combinations beginning with an א; on another a ב would be added in the same way, making a complete table of 484 triliteral combinations with the letter ב at the beginning. Proceeding thus with the remaining letters, we should get all possible triliteral combinations that can be made out of the twenty-two letters. In this way two-thirds of the labor otherwise necessary is saved, for adding the third letter is only one third of the labor required to produce all the triliteral combinations. Should we desire to write all the quadriliteral combinations that can be made out of the 22 letters, we have only to make twenty-two copies of all the triliteral combinations, leaving sufficient space between two successive combinations for the addition of a new letter; then by adding an א at the beginning of each triliteral combination, we shall attain 10,648 quadriliterals beginning with an א. Proceeding in the same way with ב, we shall obtain 10,648 quadriliterals beginning with ב, and so forth with the remaining letters, which would give a total of 22^4, or 234,256. The number of quinqueliteral combinations would amount to 22^5, or 5,153,632.

The powers of twenty-two up to 12 are as follows:

484 = 22^2
10,648 = 22^3
234,256 = 22^4
5,153,632 = 22^5
113,379,904 = 22^6
2,494,357,888 = 22^7
54,875,873,536 = 22^8
1,207,269,217,792 = 22^9
26,559,922,791,424 = 22^{10}
584,318,501.411,328 = 22^{11}
12,855,002,631,049,216 = 22^{12}

Thus it is evident that the twenty-two letters will admit of an infinity of combinations and arrangements, sufficient to represent not only all conceptions of the mind, but all words in all languages whatever.

The same results would be obtained, according to the Sefer Yetzirah, by adding a letter at the end of each combination. When a letter is added at the beginning, the process is called

וחוזר הגלגל פנים, the table "turns" in front of each letter, as נג "turning" in front of the ע becomes ענג, and when a letter is added at the end, it is called וחוזר הגלגל אחור, the table "turns" behind each letter, as נג turning behind the ע becomes נגע. Thus, as either ענג or נגע can be formed from the combination נג by adding an ע, so all the triliteral combinations can be made out of the biliteral combinations, by adding an additional letter, either at the beginning or at the end of the biliteral combinations, and the quadriliterals from the triliterals, etc., without the necessity of writing the letters anew, when new combinations are desired.

How infinite numbers of words are formed out of the twenty-two letters, the Sefer Yetzirah demonstrates by permutations in which letters never repeat themselves but only change their places. Out of two letters[6]) two biliteral words are formed as: אב, בא Out of three letters six triliteral words are formed as: אבג, אגב, באג, בגא, גאב, גבא. Out of four letters 24 quadriliteral words are formed as: אבגד, אבדג, אגבד, אגדב, אדבג, אדגב, באגד, באדג, בגאד, בגדא, בדאג, בדגא, גאבד, גאדב, גבאד, גבדא, גדאב, גדבא, דאבג, דאגב, דבאג, דבגא, דגאב, דגבא. Out of five letters 120 quinqueliteral words are formed, out of six letters 720 six-letter words are formed and out of seven letters 5,040 seven-letter words are formed. The Sefer Yetzirah gives the factorials up to that of seven and concludes the Mishnah by saying: "Go and count further, what the mouth is unable to pronounce, and the ear is unable to hear."

[6]) See text, § 8.

The factorials up to that of 12 are as follows:

1 = (1
2 = (2
6 = (3
24 = (4
120 = (5
720 = (6
5,040 = (7
40,320 = (8
362,880 = (9
3,628,800 = (10
39,916,800 = (11
479,001,600 = (12

The factorials up to 36 are given in Rees' Encyclopedia, art. *Cipher*. The Mishnah treating of permutation was well explained by all commentators, especially by S. Donnolo.

W. Stanley Jevons on the subject of permutation says[7]: "Thus the letters *A*, *B*, *C*, will make different permutations according as *A* stands first, second or third; having decided the place of *A*, there are two places between which we may choose for *B*; and then remains but one place for *C*. Accordingly, the permutation of these letters will be altogether 3 x 2 x 1 or 6 in number. With four things or letters *A*, *B*, *C*, and *D*, we shall have four choices of places for the first letter, three for the second, two for the third, and one for the fourth, so that there will be altogether 4 x 3 x 2 x 1, or 24 permutations. The same simple rule applies to all cases; beginning with the

[7]) The Principles of Science, London 1887, 173, 179.

whole number ot things, we multiply at each step by a number decreased by a unit ...."

He further says: "Many writers have from time to time remarked upon the extraordinary magnitude of the numbers with which we deal in this subject. Taqnet calculated that the twenty-four letters of the alphabet may be arranged in more than 620 thousand trillions of orders; and Schott estimated that if a thousand million of men were employed for the same number of years in writing out these arrangements, and each man filled, each day, forty pages with forty arrangements in each, they would not have accomplished the task, as they would have written only 584 thousand trillions instead of 620 thousand trillions."

CHAP. II

THE TETRAGRAMMATON AND THE VOWELS

All words arising from the combination of the letters are combined and permuted with the Tetragrammaton, called by the Sefer Yetzirah "One Name" יהוה, from which emanated the whole of creation and all languages[8]). According to the Sefer Yetzirah, the alphabet did not consist of consonants only, as is held by many Semitic scholars, but had vowels also, the letters of the Tetragrammaton themselves being vowels. Indeed, the ancients transcribed יהוה by the vowels *i-e-u-o*, and *i-a-o-u-e*[9]).

[8]) See text, § 9.
[9]) Comp. Renan, History of the People of Israel, Boston 1888. I, 69.

To understand how the letters of the Tetragammaton can be vowels, it is necessary to know what the Hebrew vowels are. Here the view of various writers differ widely. Dunash Ibn Tamim[10]), whose opinion was shared by many Hebrew writers, maintained that the three letters אוי are the original vowels of the Hebrew alphabet; Roger Bacon[11]), Masklef, and others held that the six letters אהוחיע were originally vowels; and Jerome and many others asserted that the five letters אהויע were the original vowels. In my opinion the original vowels are the four letters אעוי, which are still used as vowels in transcribing other languages in Hebrew characters. The Sefardic Jews, when writing Spanish with Hebrew letters, transcribe *a* by א; *i* and *e* by י; and *u* and *o* by ו The Ashkenazic Jews, when writing German with Hebrew letters, transcribe *a* and *o* by א, *e* by ע, *u* by ו, and *i* or *j* by י. An investigation into the relation of the letters to the vowel points according to the Ashkenazic pronunciation led me to the conclusion that ע has the sound of *a*, א of *e*, and *o*, י of *i*. and ו of *u*, besides its sounds of *w*.

If this opinion with regard to the original letters be correct, not only an א is hidden under a ה of the Tetragrammaton יהוה, as believed by Dunash Ibn Tamim,[12]) Judah ha-Levi, and Abraham Ibn Ezra, but also an ע. In order to understand the secret of the Tetragrammaton, the nature of the ה must be better defined. We have seen that many authors since Jerome

[10]) Sefer Yetzirah, London 1902, 20, 45, 48.
[11]) See *JQR.*, XV, 336.
[12]) Sefer Yetzirah, London 1902, 45.

believed ה to be a vowel. This is not the opinion of the Sefer Yetzirah. It counts ה among the simple letters, and, consequently, no sound in addition to that of *h* can be attached to it. On the other hand, the ה occurs at the end of words as silent, indicating that it occupies the place of a vowel letter. We must therefore assume that the Sefer Yetzirah considers ה to play the same part among the vowel letters as zero does among numerals. As zero is not a digit itself, but only occupies the place of a digit, so the silent ה is not a vowel itself, but merely occupies the place of a vowel. In the Tetragrammaton, both the ה after the ו and the ה after the י occupy the place of a vowel letter. The original letters of the Tetragrammaton were יעוא instead of יהוה.

Now, what is the "great secret," which the three mother letters (vowels) אמש contain according to the Sefer Yetzirah? Dunash Ibn Tamim declared it to be the three vowel letters אוי, which he identified with the Tetragrammaton יהוה the "secret name." In my opinion, אמש stands for אעו, and אמת which occurred in the Rashi text of the Sefer Yetzirah (Rashi, commentary on Job 28, 27; S. Sachs, התחיה, p. 94) stands for אעי. According to the original Sefer Yetzirah there are four mother letters, אכשר, cryptograms which should be deciphered by the letters אעוי: the א by א, the כ by the ע, the ש by the ו and the ר by the י. From these four letters emanated, according to the Sefer Yetzirah, the four elements, air, water, fire, and earth.

The Sefer Yetzirah apparently used אמשת as secret characters representing אעוי, because the Hebrew alphabet is arranged with the א at the beginning, the מ in the middle, and the ש and the ת at the end: while the Arabic alphabet was originally arranged with the א at the beginning, the ע in the middle, and the ו and י at the end. The Arabic alphabet consisted originally of the following seventeen letters:[13])

ا ب ج د ر س ص ش ع ف ق ل م ن ه و ي

א ב ג ד ר ש צ ט ע פ ב ל מ נ ה ו י

The fact that the Arabic alphabet has the א at the beginning, the ע in the middle, and the ו and the י at the

[13]) As אעו"י were originally vowels and as ה has an aspirate sound, which originally may not have been counted as a consonant, therefore there are only twelve consonant letters in this alphabet. Hugo Winckler (Die Babylonische Kultur, Leipzig 1902 (P. 47) Says: Es wurden ursprünglich zwölf nach dem Tierkreiszeichen benannte „Konsonanten" unterschieden, welche durch drei Vokale regiert werden, wie der Tierkreis durch die drei Regenten. The Hebrew letters according to the Arabic order would be as follows אבת גהדר זס שצין טעפף קכך לםם נן הוי.

If this were also the original order of the Hebrew alphabet, the א must have been at the beginning, the ע in the middle and the ו and the י at the end, instead of א at the beginning, מ in the middle, and ש and ת at the end.

Although the א has been placed at the beginning of the alphabet its two sounds e and o, however, harmonize between a and u the sounds of ע and ו respectively. מ"ם (=ע) דוממת שי"ן (=ו) שורקת ואל"ף מכריע בינתים (Text § 10). This would indicate that the author knew also of an order of the vowel letters, as עאוי = עֻאָאוֹי = i, u, o, e, a.

G. H. von Meyer (The organs of Speech, New York 1881 p. 225 says: "Czermack first showed that the elevation of the soft palate differed with the utterance of each vowel, the greatest elevation occurring with the vowel i (ee in see) and that the elevation gradually diminished when the vowels were uttered in the following order: i, u, o, e, a." The Sefer Yetzira seems to be of the same opinion.

end, leads to the conclusion that the arrangement of the Arabic alphabet is older than that of the Hebrew, although the contrary is generally believed to be the case.

The alphabet was anciently believed to symbolize the whole universe. The vowels which were the original letters of the Tetragrammaton, were placed at the beginning, in the middle, and at the end of the alphabet, to signify that יהוה is the God of the whole universe, that He is the beginning, the middle, and the end.

According to their sounds, we may count, in the Hebrew alphabet, thirty-two letters, divided into five vowels (ע = *a*, א = *e*, א = *o*, ו = *u*, י = *i*) and twenty-seven consonants. Each vowel, according to the Sefer Yetzirah (see text, § 12), stands by itself, but the consonants are dependent on the vowels. The vowels and consonants were made in the form of a "state and arranged like an army in battle array." Isaac Taylor[14] says: "Like soldiers on parade the characters in the alphabetic line have been dressed."

CHAP. III.

SEFIROT.

The origin of the alphabet was, and still is, a burning question to scholars. Did it spring from the Egyptian hieroglyphics, or from the cuneiform systems of the Assyrians, or from the hieroglyphics of the Hittites, or from the Syllabary

14) The Alphabet, London 1883, I, 125.

of Cyprus? The Sefer Yetzirah answers: "From the Sefirot"[15]). But what does it mean by Sefirot? On this point endless discussions arose; and it has even been disputed whether they are designed to express theological, philosophical, or physical mysteries. Most of the writers, bent on explaining the Sefer Yetzirah in a philosophical way, maintain that by עשר ספירות בלימה, the Sefer Yetzirah meant the so-called Arabic numerals, 1, 2, 3, 4, 5, 6, 7, 8, 9, and 0. This view is shared by Dunash Ibn Tamim[16]), who, however, admits that some people object to it, and maintain that if the Sefer Yetzirah had meant the Arabic numerals, it would have said תשע ספירות (nine Sefirot): for as the cipher is not a digit, there are only nine significant numbers. A much weightier reason for opposing the identification of the Sefirot with the Arabic numerals is the fact that the Sefer Yetzirah gives ten as the total number resulting from the addition of the numerals 1, 2, 3 and 4, and the total of the 9 Arabic numerals added together is 45.

However, there can be no doubt that the Sefirot philosophy of the Sefer Yetzirah rested on some system of numeral notation. I have studied various systems of antiquity and I have found that it harmonizes with a numeral system consisting of a series of strokes from one to four, amounting in all to ten | || ||| ||||, and the zero 0. Indeed, the numbers 1, 2, 3, and 4 were originally indicated by such a series of strokes, as is well known to all familiar with the old Roman, Greek, and South-Arabian systems of notation. The numeral

[15]) See text, § 14.

[16]) See Sefer Yeṣirah, London 1902, 24, 25.

systems of the Phœnicians, Egyptians, Babylonians etc., even indicated the numbers 5, 6, 7, 8 and 9 by the first four groups of strokes, as || ||| = 5, ||| ||| = 6, | ||| ||| = 7, || ||| ||| = 8, and ||| ||| ||| = 9. There can be no doubt, therefore, that by עשר ספירות the Sefer Yetzirah meant 1, 2, 3, and 4 written in strokes, their number amounting, when added together, to ten [17]), and by בלימה it meant zero, which, being a symbol for nothing, is the equivalent of בלימה, "nothing" in Hebrew. My belief is that originally the text must have had עשר ספירות ובלימה = ten digits and zero.

As, according to the Sefer Yetzirah, it is possible to express all numbers by the ten Sefirot [18]), we must demonstrate how all numbers, even those higher than nine, may be indicated by the ten strokes. The strokes to indicate numbers were anciently written vertically and horizontally as — = ≡ ≣. By means of the strokes and the zero, all numbers may be expressed, as they are expressed by the Arabic numerals. The numbers 10, 20, 30, 40, 50....500...5000....50000 may be expressed as — 0, = 0, ≡ 0, ≣ 0, ≣ 0, ... ≣ 00, ≣ 000, ≣ 0000.

1907 for instance would be represented thus: — ≣ 0 ≣ [19]).

[17]) Dr. H. Malter calls my attention to the following passage of Abraham Abulafia in Jellinek's גנזי חכמת הקבלה, Leipzig 1853, p. 20: מוחו של תינוק סופר עשר ספירות שהם נבללין בארבע לפי צורות האצילות בדרך זו א״ב ג״ד אשר האצילות נאצלית משם בזו (כאלו נכתבו יוד אלפי הה אחר הה). This passage proves that the true meaning of the Sefirot had been known to some Hebrew writers.

[18]) See text, § 16.

[19]) Some Pythagoreans used the strokes with the principle of position without a zero in the columns of an abacus (Dr. M. Cantor's *Mathematische Beiträge*, page 202).

Such a system of notation is practically the abacus on paper and apparently was the source of the scientific system of notation of the Chinese, and may have been the source of the Arabic numerals, the origin of which is admittedly doubtful. To avoid writing too many strokes, the Chinese made one stroke to represent five units. The numerals 1, 2, 3, 4, 5, 6, 7, 8, 9, 0, were written, |, ||, |||, ||||, |||||, T, TT, TTT, TTTT, 0. 1405536 for instace was written | ≣ 0 ≣ ||||| ═ T (see M. Cantor's Mathematische Beiträge. Halle 1863, 46 and 47; first table figures 15, 16).

The East-Arabian figures ١, ٢, ٣, ٤ (1, 2, 3, and 4) originated from the primitive numerals | || ||| ||||. They are only a combination of two, three, and four strokes, to indicate the respective numbers. The figure ٥ for 5 originated from the circle, which in the primitive system of numeral notation was the fifth symbol representing a zero, and in the South-Arabian system of numeral notation was a symbol representing ten units. The East-Arabian figures, ٦, ٧. ٨ (6, 7, and 8) are each a combination of two strokes. The figure ٩ originated apparently from a circle and a stroke, and a dot indicated a zero.

Many writers maintain that only at a later period the principle of position and the zero was discovered. We are, however, now certain that in Babylon, many centuries before the Christian Era. a sexagesimal position was known. In my opinion, the sexagesimal position originated from the decimal position, and not the reverse; for the earliest abacus, which was doubtless based on a decimal position, is older than the sexagesimal system. F. Cajori says:[20]) "The principle of position in its general and systematic application required a symbol for zero. We ask, Did the Babylonians possess one? Had they already taken the gigantic step of representing by a symbol the absence of units?" I am inclined to believe that the zero is as old as the principle of position[21]). The final perfection of the so-called Arabic system of notation consisted, not in the discovery of the principle of position and the zero, but rather in pointing out how the primitive principle of position and the zero can be conveniently used with nine figures, such as 1, 2, 3, 4, 5, 6, 7, 8, and 9.

Although the sexagesimal position was anciently known in Babylonia, yet it was used only, in higher mathematics, as in

[20]) A History of Mathematics, New York 1894, p. 7.

[21]) In the *American Mathematical Monthly*, 1909, p 177, G. A. Miller calls attention to the recent change of view in reference to several important questions in the history of elementary mathematics. On page 576 of Cantor's *Vorlesungen über Geschichte der Mathematik* (second edition, vol. I), the following words are found: "According to our opinion the discovery of zero is due to the Hindoos." The corresponding statement in the third edition, page 616, reads as follows: "According to our opinion the discovery is due to the Babylonians, the deepening of the concept is due to the Hindoos." G. A. Miller further says: "The discovery of zero, as used above, implies its use in positional arithmetic. It is certain that the Greeks employed zero in the second century B. C. to denote the absence of degrees, minutes, or seconds in their sexagesimal notation. The earliest known use of this symbol in Babylonian inscriptions belongs to the third century B. C., but it is supposed that it was in use at a much earlier date. At the International Mathematical Congress held in Paris in 1900, Cantor suggested that zero was probably in use among the Babylonians as early as 1700 B. C. Even if such an early date cannot be established, it appears likely that scholars will hereafter attribute the discovery of positional arithmetic to the Babylonians instead of the Hindoos."

astronomy, etc.; for ordinary purposes there was a decimal system of notation, without the principle of position. When we find that in Egypt and Phœnicia only a decimal system of notation was used, without the principle of position, it may not be taken as proof that the decimal position and zero were unknown. A decimal system of notation without the principle of position was in ancient times considered more convenient than a decimal system of notation based upon the principle of position.

When it was, that the primitive numerals, |, ||, |||, ||||, o, were changed into the figures used by the East-Arabs, to indicate the numbers 1, 2, 3, 4, 5, 6, 7, 8, and 9. I shall not venture to conjecture. But it is proper to assume, that they may have been known to a few learned men long before they began to be widely used. They may have even been known to the author of the Sefer Yetzirah[22]). Yet by ישר

24) As an early Arabian mathematician Mohammed ben Musa Alkhowarezmi said that the Indians practiced the so-called Arabian system of notation (M. Cantor's *Mathematische Beiträge*, Halle 1863, page 269), arguments have been advanced that the Indians invented this system, or at least taught it to the Arabs. But it is very doubtful what Mohammed ben Musa meant by Indians. By Indians he might have meant Ethiopians, or any other nation under the torrid zone which the ancients used to denominate as Indians (T. Astle, The Origin and Progress of Writing, London 1784, p. 41; השלח, IX, 354, 439). Or he could have meant Jewish astronomers like Mashallah, who was called by Abraham ibn Ezra an Indian sage (חכם הודו) (see M. Steinschneider, *Arab. Literatur der Juden*, Frankf. a.M. 1902, p. 15) As the Arabic numeral system of notation apparently originated from the Sefirot philosophy of the Sefer Yetzirah, it is proper to share the view of those who claim the Hebrews as its inventors (E. Brooks, the Philosophy of Arithmetic, Philadelphia 1876, p. 24).

ספירות בלימה the author meant, not the Arabic numerals, but the primitive numerals, |, ||, |||, ||||, 0, from which the Arabic numerals originated.

As, according to the Sefer Yetzirah, the alphabet originated from the ten Sefirot, which are, as was demonstrated, the first four groups of strokes amounting to ten, we must assume that the first alphabet must have been constructed out of these strokes. This peculiarity harmonizes best with the Libyan-Berberic alphabet, in which we actually find each of the first four groups of strokes: —, =, ≡, ≣, |, ||, |||, |||| and the circle ○ or ⊙ is each a letter. Moreover, the other letters of the same alphabet have such forms as point, without a doubt, to their origin in the first four groups of strokes, | || ||| ||||. Two, three, or four strokes are so combined as to indicate the various letters as: 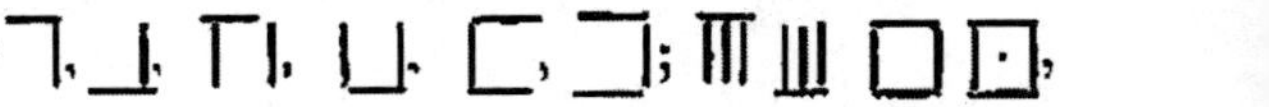 etc.[23]).

Similar to these characters are the linear letters, which have been found on the Egyptian pottery. On this subject, Mr. W. J. Harding King[24]) says: "Mr. Evans and Professor Flinders Petrie have shown that certain linear characters which have been found on the Egyptian pottery ...... form a signary in which a large number of the characters are identical with the Libyan and Tifinagh. The linear characters in Egypt are earlier than the hieroglyphics, though a few of the forms may ultimately have been fused with the latter. Evolved at a

[23]) K. Faulmann, *Geschichte der Schrift*, Wien 1880, p. 257. Bickell, Hebrew Grammar, Leipzig 1877. Table of Semitic characters by Julius Euting, No. 52, 53.

[24]) A Search for the Masked Tawareks, London 1903, p. 322.

date when hieroglyphic writing was unknown, they persisted with a strange vitality, and were never absorbed or ousted." It is proper to note that, in some Berberic alphabets[25]), one, two, three, or four dots are placed in various positions, to indicate different letters. The four groups of dots . .. .:.., which may be arranged in triangular form .·∴·.·., as the Pythagoreans arranged them, were originally also symbols representing the first four numbers 1, 2, 3, and 4[26]). As already demonstrated, the first alphabet invented was similar to that still used by the Berbers, whence the inference, that there may have been a time when the Hebrews also used such an alphabet. May not כתב ליבונאה[27]) originally have meant Libyan writing?

According to J. Halévy's decipherment of the Libyan alphabet | or — is א, || or = is ו, ||| or ≡ is י, |||| is ה. According to the Sefer Yetzirah (§§ 10, 11, 18, 19, 20, 21) | or — is א, || or = is י, ||| or ≡ is ו, |||| or ≣ is ה. Hence, the vowel-letters אוי were originally indicated by the four groups amounting to ten strokes, |, ||, |||, |||| or — = ≡ ≣. If these vowel sounds were originally the numeral words for one, two, three, and four, we may assume that the vowel symbols were invented at the same time as the numerals. The invention of such an alphabet as the Libyan must have consisted, chiefly of symbols for consonants, because vowel sym-

[25]) K. Faulman, p. 257–8.

[26]) Cyrus Thomas in the 19th Annual Report of the Bureau of American Ethnology, Smithsonian Institution, 1897–98, p. 860.

[27]) Sanhedrin 21b.

bols were already in existence from the time the numerals were invented.

In this way we can understand why the vowels (the Tetragammaton) were originally identical with the ten digits עשר ספירות, | || ||| ||||. This is also in harmony with the following quotations from the commentary (אוצר ה'[28]): "In His great name which is Jehovah, בשמו הגדול הוא הויה, for He comprises the Ten Sefirot." כי הוא הכולל לכל י' ספירות. "When it mentions the 'mothers' (vowels) it means the Seifirot themselves." כשהזכיר אמות מדבר בעצמי הספירות "It was explained in the second chapter that, wherever it says 'mothers,' it alludes to the Sefirot themselves." כבר פירש' בפ"ב כי כל מקום שאמר אמות ירמוז לעצמי הספירות.

The four elements, air, water, fire, and earth, from which it was anciently believed everything was created, emanated, according to the Sefer Yetzirah, from the vowels אעוי; air emanated from the א, water from the ע, fire from the ו and earth from the י. As the vowels were originally identical with the ten Sefirot, it is from the Sefirot that the whole universe emanated[29]). The Sefirot cosmogony is given by the Sefer Yetzirah as follows:

„With 'one,' the living God of the Universe graved and hewed out voice, air, and speech, and this is the Holy Spirit. With 'two' God graved and hewed out void and chaos. Void is a green line that surrounds the whole universe, and chaos refers to viscous stones, sunk in the abyss, whence water comes forth."

[28]) *Sefer Yetzirah*, Warsaw 1884, p. 69, 74, 90.
[29]) See text, § 17.

„With 'three' God graved and hewed out mud and clay. He arranged them like a garden bed. He set them up like a wall. He covered them like a pavement, and poured upon them snow, and the earth was formed."

"With 'four' God graved and hewed out the Throne of Glory, the ophanim, the seraphim, the holy animals, and the ministering angels"[30]).

Chaos signified in the ancient cosmogonies the vacant, infinite space out of which sprang all things that exist. Later cosmogonists, such as Ovid, represent it as the confused, shapless mass, out of which the universe was formed into a cosmos, or harmonious order. W. Enfield[31]) says: "By Chaos some writers understood water, and make this the first material principle". He further says:[32]) "The theogonists certainly do not suppose God to have been prior in the order of time to matter: they speak of Chaos as eternal, and seem to have been wholly unacquainted with the doctrine of creation from nothing". This is at variance with the Sefer Yetzirah, which emphasizes the doctrine of creation from nothing by the statement: "He (God) formed existence out of void, something out of nothing" (Mishnah 22). It holds that chaos was not even the first thing created, but was preceded by voice, air, and speech[33]).

30) See text, §§ 18–21.

31) History of Philosophy, London 1819, I, 180.

32) *Ibid.*, 131.

33) The number philosophy of Pythagoras has been explained (W. Enfield, History of Philosophy London, 1819 vol. I. p. 383) as follows: „Intelligible numbers are those which subsisted in the divine mind before all things, from which everything has received its form, and which always remain immutably the same. It is the model, or archetype, after

The numeral system of the Sefer Yetzirah, as I have explained, may be considered to consist of five symbols, |, ||, |||, ||||, 0, the cipher being the fifth symbol. From this symbol originated the numeral O (5) in the East-Arabian notation. It is identical in form with the letter ه (ה) of the Arabic alphabet. As the ה indicates the absence of a vowel letter, and is similar in its nature to the zero, which indicates the absence of a digit, it is possible that the ה originated from the zero. The first primitive numerals |, ||, |||, ||||, 0, were thus primarily identical. with the five vowel-letters אהוי which were originally the letters of the Tetragrammaton יהוה. The five primitive symbols are the five elements with which God created

which the world. in all its parts, is framed. Numbers are the cause of essence to beings . . . The Monad, or unity, is that quantity which, being deprived of all number, remains fixed: whence called Monad. It is the fountain of all numbers. The Duad is imperfect and passive, and the cause of increase and division. The Triad, composed of the Monad and Duad, partakes of the nature of both. The Tetrad, Tetractys, quaternian number, is the most perfect. The Decad, which is the sum of the four former, comprehends all arithmetical and musical proportions. According to some writers, the Monad denotes the active principle of nature, or God: the Duad, the passive principle or mother: the Triad, the world (in the Sefer Yetzira, the earth) formed by the union of the two former: and the Tetractys, the perfection of nature. Some have understood by this mysterious number the four elements; others, the four faculties of the human mind; others, the four cardinal virtues; and others have been so absurd as to suppose Pythagoras made use of this number to express the name of God, in reference to the word יהוה, by which that name is expressed in the Hebrew language. But every attempt to unfold this mystery has hitherto been unsuccessful".

The reader will find below my view on the origin of the Pythagorean philosophy. I will only say here that there is no absurdity in identifying the Tetractys with the Tetragrammaton; and moreover the identity is established by the Sefer Yetzirah.

the universe, the ה or the zero being the fifth element, as the Sefer Yetzirah says:[34]) יצר מתהו ממש ועשה אינו ישנו וחצב אבנים גדולות מאויר שאינו נתפש וסימן לדבר עשרים ושתים מנין ורוח אחד.

"He formed existence out of void, something out of nothing, and He hewed large stones out of intangible air, thus, twenty-two in number, one in spirit."

The word תהו (void) has the same meaning as בלימה; it is also equivalent to zero, which symbolizes the creation of something out of nothing. This is in accordance with the teaching of the Pythagoreans who counted the void surrounding the universe as a fifth element (Wilhelm Bauer, *Der ältere Pythagoreismus*, Berne 1897, pp. 83, 84, 88, 89).

We must conclude that the so-called Arabic numerals and the alphabet originated from the ten digits and the zero, or rather from two symbols, 1 0, the stroke and the circle. L. D. Nelme[35]), in his essay on the origin of letters, shows that all

[34]) See text, § 22.

[35]) Comp. "An Essay towards an Investigation of the Origin and Elements of Language and Letters" by L. D. Nelme, London 1762. On page 16 we read as follows: "All his (Gods) creation, and every minutest part thereof, participates of two most essential forms; the line 1 the symbol of the altitude, and the circle 0 the symbol of the horizon. These symbols contain in them the first elements, the forms of all created nature. There doth not exist in the whole creation any being, or thing, that doth not partake of the first principles; nor can the human mind conceive of any existence, without ideas that include these first elements; which are not only forms essential to all matter but also to every idea of matter that arises in the human mind: they contain in them the elements of every art, and of every science known to man; and they are the radix of letters also, which we have already considered as symbols expressive of ideas."

elementary characters, or letters, derive their forms from the line and the circle. As I understand the Sefer Yetzirah, it also holds that all written characters originated from a line and a circle, but from a line that was originally a symbol for unity, and a circle that was originally the symbol for zero. Similarly, all cuneiform characters originated from two symbols Y < those for one and ten.

L. L. Conant[36] says: "Two centuries ago the distinguished philosopher and mathematician Leibnitz proposed a binary system of numeration, the only symbols needed in such a system would be 0 and | . . . Leibnitz found in the representation of all numbers by means of two digits 0 and | a fitting symbolization of the Creation out of chaos or nothing, of the Universe by the power of the Deity." We have seen that not only a binary system of numeration, but even the decimal system may be expressed by a stroke and a zero. Moreover, it has been pointed out that the alphabet and the so-called Arabic numerals originated from these two symbols. Therefore, the author of the Sefer Yetzirah may have meant by two , with which God created void and chaos, a digit and a zero; for as the ten digits may be expressed by nine digits and a zero, so may two digits be represented by a digit and a zero. Thus, the Sefer Yetzirah may have believed two digits, o and | , a fitting symbolization of the creation, out of chaos or nothing, of the universe, by the power of the Deity.

Because the zero in the number ten occupies the space of a digit, only nine strokes, not ten, are used; and, therefore, we

36) The Number Concept, New York 1896, p. 102.

may say that the numeral system of the Sefer Yetzirah, consists of nine digits and the zero. For | || ||| |||| 0 = ||||||||| 0, and the symbol ⚹ expresses the whole numeral system. The latter figure was anciently known in South Arabia, and it represented, according to Halévy, an ע[37]. The Sefer Yetzirah calls the letters "stones" (אבנים), because they originated from the numerals (Sefirot), which were originally indicated by stones. It is possible, therefore, that the ⚹ is the philosopher's stone, from which the Arabic numerals, the alphabet, and all civilization originated.

Moreover, since in ⚹ are united the ten Sefirot, the vowels and the Tetragrammaton, it apparently symbolized the angel containing the name יהוה, referred to in Exodus 23, 20, 21. This angel is chiefly known in kabbalistic literature by the name מטטרון שר הפנים "Metatron, Prince of the Face" and is identified with the prophet Elijah[38]. He is the שר היצירה "Prince of Creation," or the „Logos," with which God created the universe. Upon the crown of the head of this angel "The Holy one — Blessed be He" wrote letters with which were created heaven, earth, seas, rivers, etc., and all the elements of creation[39]. To this angel God intrusted all the secrets of the Law, and of wisdom; and all the mysteries of creation are known to him as they are known to the Creator Himself[40]. As the Arabic numeral system of notation, the vowels, and the

37) Comp. D. H. Müller, *Epigraphische Denkmäler aus Arabien*, Vienna 1889, p. 19.

38) ילקוט ראובני. Lemberg 1860, p. 47b.

39) *Ibid.*, 52b.

40) *Ibid*, 48b

Tetragrammaton were originally identical, they all contain the same 'great secret' the revelation of which is forbidden by the author of the Sefer Yetzirah (text, §§ 10, 11, 14). This secret apparently is the angel

אליהו הנביא = מטטרון שר הפנים

symbolized by the letter ה, which was anciently written also as ✳.

The most mysterious character in Jewish history is the prophet Elijah. It was he who demonstrated that יהוה is the true God and no other. He is called the angel of the Covenant, מלאך הברית. He is believed to be present at the circumcision. It is also believed that he is bound to come and decide all knotty points in the law, and to appear before the true Messiah arrives.

In kabbalistic literature, not only the vowel letter ה, but all the letters are considered images of angels. In Sefer Raziel (ed. Amsterdam, p. 126) occurs the following:

כארם שחקק אותיות מן דמות אותם המלאכים שנטרדו וגער בהם הקב"ה והפילם משמי מרום ושב וחקק את דמותם מאלף ועד תי"ו.

"Like Adam who engraved letters out of the likeness ot those angels who had been driven away, whom the Holy One, Blessed be He, rebuked and cast down from the high heavens. He then graved their likeness from Aleph to Taw."

The vowel letters, however, the letters of the Tetragrammaton, are images and pictures of superior angels. Since the cipher ה is also a letter of the Tetragrammaton, it is also a picture and image of a superior angel. The angel which the cipher ה symbolizes, is apparently Satan שטן, who appears before God to prosecute all mortal beings as he prosecuted

Job and Joshua son of Jehozadak (Job 1, 6—12: 2, 1—7; Zechar. 3, 1). Like the cipher ה so the zero in the Arabic system of notation, and in the system from which the latter originated, was anciently believed to symbolize the evil deity, or Satan[41]), in contrast to the numeral one 1, which was thought to symbolize the good God, from whom all good emanated. The numeral one 1 and the zero 0 are a fitting symbolization of the two opposing principles concerning which the Sefer Yetzirah (§ 23) says as follows:

"Also God set the one over against the other, good against evil, and evil against good: good out of good; and evil out of evil; good testing evil, and evil testing good; good is stored away for the good, and evil is stored away for the evil."

The account of the origin of letters and numerals the author of the Sefer Yetzirah concludes as follows:

"When Abraham our father arose, he looked and saw and investigated and observed and engraved and hewed and combined and formed and calculated, and his creation was successful. Then the Master of all revealed himself to him, and made a

41) "It was not very easy to comprehend at first the precise force of the cipher, which, insignificant by itself, only serves to determine the rank and value of the other digits. A sort of mystery, which has imprinted its trace on language, seemed to hang over the practice of numeration, for we still speak of deciphering, and of writing in cipher, in allusion to some dark or concealed art" (The Philosophy of Arithmetic, by John Leslie, Edinburgh 1817, p. 114). "Indeed, in the early history of arithmetic in Europe . . . . the system was regarded as belonging to black art and the devil: and it was, no doubt, this popular prejudice that delayed its general introduction into Christian Europe" (E Brooks, The Philosophy of Arithmetic, Philadelphia 1901, p. 107).

covenant with him and with his seed forever. He made a covenant with him on the ten fingers of his hands, and this is the covenant of the tongue; and on the ten toes of his feet, and this is the covenant of circumcision; and tied the twenty-two letters of the "Torah" to his tongue and revealed to him their secret..."

The name of Abraham which is mentioned in the closing Mishnah suggested to many commentators that Abraham himself wrote the Sefer Yetzirah. As such a view is entirely repugnant to the modern critical mind, some writers regard this closing Mishnah as a later interpolation. In my opinion there is no doubt that this Mishnah belongs to the original Sefer Yetzirah, for it is in perfect harmony with all the original material. The mention of the name of Abraham does not indicate that the Patriarch wrote the Sefer Yetzirah, but that he was the inventor of the alphabet, the scribe (סופר) mentioned in the opening Mishnah as the person whom God inspired with it.

It is worthy of note that Philo attributes the first invention of letters to Abraham (Rees, *Cyclopedia*, art. *Letter*; comp. also Suidas in Abraham and Isidor Hispal, Origg, 1, 3).

CHAP. IV.

THE TEXT.

No Hebrew book has been so tampered with as the Sefer Yetzirah. As early as the tenth century there existed several versions of it, varying in length and in arrangement. There were the short and the long version, which were edited in Mantna in 1562, and Saadia's text, edited by M. Lambert, in Paris, in 1891. Each of these three texts is different trom the others. Although Saadia's version is almost ot the same length as Mantua II, it differs materially therefrom in the arrangement of the chapters and the paragraphs, and it thus happens that the matter contained in one chapter in Mantua II may be found scattered through several chapters in Saadia's text: while entire paragraphs in Saadia's text are cut up and distribnted among three different chapters in Mantua II. Both Mantua texts agree in a general way with each other in their arrangement, but Mantua II contains twice as much material as Mantua I, the former numbering about 2400 words, the latter only 1200 words.

A critical study leads to the conclusion that these versions contain only obouth 600 words of the original Sefer Yetzirah. The remaining 600 words in Mantua I or the 1800 words in Mantna II are all interpolations and not of the original Sefer Yetzirah. All the matter belonging to the original Sefer Yetzirah, I arranged as a separate treatise, which may be reffered to as Sefer Yetzirah I. All the interpolations I arranged also as a separate treatise, which may be referred to as Sefer Yetzirah II. Having already explained the Sefer Yetzirah I, it now remains to explain the Sefer Yetzirah II.

Of the Sefer Yetzirah II little need be said; it abounds in trifles, contradictions and repetitions. Although it was intended as a commentary on Sefer Yetzirah I, its author had no conception whatever of what the original Sefer Yetzirah was. He saw in it only a cosmogony based upon the letters of the alphabet and the Sefiroth. According to him God created the universe with thirty-two wonderful ways of wisdom. These ways are the ten Sefiroth and the twenty-two letters. The ten Sefiroth are: The Spirit of God, Air. Water, Fire, Height, Depth, East, West, North, and South. From the first emanated the second: from the second the third, from the third the fourth, and the remaining six sefiroth emanated from the six permutations of the letters יהו. With the second Sefirah (Air) God created the twenty-two letters, and divided them into thre parts, or books (שלשה ספרים): three mothers אמש: seven double letters בג״ד כפר״ת, and twelve simple letters: הוז חטי לנס עצק.

With these three classes, or groups, of letters were created the various parts of the world (עולם), of the year (שנה) and of the soul. (נפש).

The author of the Sefer Yetzirah II contradicts himself: he explains that by the three mother letters, אמש, which the original Sefer Yetzirah declares to be a "great secret" (סוד גדול) are meant the letters יהו of the great name יהו״ה; the mothers thus not being a separate class at all but part of the simple letters.

As a matter of fact, he himself abandons the division of the letters into three parts, and rearranges them in a twofold division, one of ten and one of twelve letters. For, finally, he counts the letters אמש with the seven double letters בגד כפרת, as one class. The whole theory of the world, of the year, and of the soul, is expressed by tens and twelves. Indeed he says[42]) as follows:

[42]) Mantua II chap VI Sepher Yetzirah II, chap. V.

עולם ספירתו בעשרה ושנים עשר . . . .
שנה ספירתה בעשרה ושנים עשר . . . .
נפש ספירתה בעשרה ושנים עשר . . . .

The world is countet by ten and twelve . . . .
The year is counted by ten and twelve . . . .
The soul is counted by ten and twelve . . . .

It therefore follows that, according to the author of the Sefer Yetzirah II, the twenty-two letters are divided into ten double אמ״ש, בגד כפרת and twelve simple letters הוז חטי לנם עצק. According to the author of the Sefer Yetzirah II, however, each double letter represents only one way of wisdom, as each simple letter does. The twenty-two letters, therefore, are, according to him, only twenty-two ways of wisdom. The remaining ten ways of wisdom are the ten Sefiroth, which he explained to be the Spirit of God, air, water, fire. height, depth, east, west. north. and south. The author of the Sefer Yetzirah II understood the numeral words. . אחת . . . שתים . . . שלש . . . ארבע. occurring in the original Sefer Yetzirah, to mean first, second, third and fourth. He imagined that the author of the original Sefer Yetzirah had counted only four Sefiroth, and had forgotten to count the remaining six Sefiroth, and after explaining that the four Sefiroth are the Spirit ot God, air, water, and fire, he counted height, depth, east, west, north, and south as six Sefiroth to complete the number of the ten Sefiroth. The truth is that the numerals אחת . . . . שתים . . . . שלש . . . . ארבע . . . mean. not first, second, third and fourth, but one, two, three and four, and these numbers themselves are the ten Sefiroth from which all letters of the alphabet (particularly the vowel letters) originated. The Sefiroth, therefore, cannot be counted as ten separate ways of wisdom. The latter view requires that the twenty-two letters shall be taken to be all the thirty-two ways of wisdom, not only twenty-two ways of wisdom as explained by the Sefer Yetzirah II which is followed by all commentators.

CHAP. V.

Saadia, who was the first to divide the letters into five groups אחהע, בומפ, גיכק, דטלנת, זסשרץ, believed all the letters to be consonants. He interpolated this division in the Sefer Yetzirah without knowing that by אמות the original Sefer Yetzirah meant vowels. The first to perceive that אמות means vowels was Dunash Ibn Tamim [43]), who explained that by the three mother letters אמש the Sefer Yezirah meant the three vowel letters אוי. He failed, however, to see that by way of contrast תולדות must necessarily mean consonants. Now, he knew that his version of the Sefer Yetzirah contained many mistakes, that ignorant people had blended the original and an early commentary [44]), and consequently the original text did not exist. Yet he did not perceive the absurdity of the division of the letters into three classes named: three mother letters אמש, seven double letters בגד כפרת and twelve simple letters הו חטי לנס עצק. The category ‚mothers‘ (אמות) is not in any sense coordinate

[43]) „Sefer Yetzirah", London, 1902, p. 45

[44]) Ibid., p. 65.

with that of "double letters" and "simple letters", which contrast admirably with each other. Moreover, he failed to perceive that according to the Sefer Yetzirah, there are ten double letters and not only seven. He is also at variance with all the known versions of the text, which give twelve simple letters, while he, in counting the total number of sounds 29, of which 14 are contained in the seven double letters בגד כפרת, makes the simple letters number 15. Besides, it is very hard to understand how Dunash could have counted the letters אוי as simple letters having one sound, and declare at the same time that originally they were vowels and consequently must have had several sounds: namely י the sounds of i and e: ו of w, u and o; א of a and other vowel sounds.

Long before I ever saw the Sefer Yetzirah, I had concluded that the Hebrew alphabet consisted of ten letters with double sounds and twelve letters with simple sounds: thus representing thirty-two sounds. I came to this conclusion in investigating the pronunciation of the vowels, which the reader will find in my לתקון הנגוד והקריאה (will appear shortly), in which I have discussed it at length. The then double letters are:

א, בּ, גּ, ד, ו, כּ, פּ, ר, שׁ, ת,

and the twelve simple letters are:

ה, ז, ח, ט, י, ל, מ, נ, ס, ע, צ, ק.

I base this division on the assumption that the letters אעוי are the original vowels of the Hebrew alphabet, and that the true sounds of these letters were as follows: ע = a, א = e, א = o, י = i, וּ = u, ו = v. Hence, the letters וא are also double letters, so that these together with the six letters בגד כפת, the letter ר and the letter ש were known to be double letters: hence, ten letters with double sounds. After reaching this conclusion, I found that the division of the letters of the Sefer Yetzirah bore a decided similarity to it. In fact, the Sefer Yetzirah gives the same number and the same classification of the single letters; the only difference is that it counts the י among the simple letters, while I considered the י as a double letter, and gave instead the מ. Nevertheless, I do not believe from a grammatical point of view, that the author of the original Sefer Yetzirah could have counted the letter י as a simple letter instead of the letter מ, and could have counted only seven double letters without including at least the letter ש which is still pronounced as a double letter by a great majority of the Jewish people. Further investigation proved that anciently there were counted ten double letters.

As is well-known, some old grammarians, among whom was the author of the "Dikduke ha-Teamim" counted the final letters as separate letters, thus making the total number of the letters of the alphabet twenty-seven. This calculation harmonizes with the statement of the Talmud and Midrash that the letters אמת form respectively the beginning, the middle, and the end of the alphabet [45], which can be true only if we count the finals as separate letters and thus make the total number twenty-seven, for otherwise the מ can not be in the middle of the alphabet. Some grammarians, though they do not consider the finals as separate letters, yet count the letters twenty-

[45]) According to Rashi, Job XXVIII, 27 the word אמת occurred in the Sefer Yetzirah: comp. above p. 17.

nine, figuring the double letters בגד כפרת and the ר or the ש as fourteen letters. Convinced that there are ten double letters and twelve simple letters, I concluded that there must have been a time when the Hebrew alphabet was reckoned thirty-two letters without the final letters, and thirty-seven or thirty-nine with the final letters, as follows:

אבבגגדדההווזחטיככךלמםנןסעפפףצץקררששתת

In such an arrangement of the letters, not the מ but the letter ל is in the middle of the alphabet.

On reaching this conclusion, I sought to find some authority in the ancient literature for placing the ל in the middle of the alphabet. This fact, if established, would prove the correctness of my views on the Hebrew vowel points and their relation to the vowel letters אהו״י as explained in לתקון הנקוד והקריאה and it would also prove that the original Sefer Yetzirah gave the number of double sound letters as ten, and not seven. To my great delight, I found, in the אותיות דרבי עקיבא the following: "Why is the letter ל higher than the other letters? Because it is in the middle of the letters". I also found in the Midrash Tadshe [46]), that the letter ל is in the middle of the letters. These passages make it clear that the ancients counted ten double letters, and in their arrangement of the alphabet, they sometimes counted them as twenty [47]).

[46]) Epstein, מקדמוניות היהודים. Wien 1887 p. XVIII

[47]) The philosopher and Grammarian Profiat Duran "Ma'ase Efod" p. 34) also says that the ancients divided the twenty-two letters of the Hebrew alphabet into ten and twelve, according to the ten spheres (גלגלים) and the twelve signs of the zodiac (מזלות).

This seemed to justify my reading of the ten double letters עשר כפולות א ב ג ד ו כ פ ר ש ת in the Sefer Yetzirah, and not seven, and my contention that by the thirty-two mysterious ways are meant the thirty-two sounds of the Hebrew alphabet, consisting ot ten double letters and twelve simple letters.

CHAP. VI

AUTHORSHIP.

Thus far, it has been impossible to determine the age and authorship of the Sefer Yetzirah. Jewish tradition claims divine origin for it: it was intrusted by the Lord to Adam and afterwards to Abraham[48]). A very interesting passage concerning Abraham and his relation to the Sefer Yetzirah is quoted by Judah Barseloni, in his commentary on the Sefer Yetzirah (p. 268), from an ancient text.

מצינו בנוסחא דראשונים הכי:

וכשנולד אברהם אבינו אמרו מלאכי השרת לפני הקב"ה רבונו של עולם אהוב יש לך בעולם ותכסה אותו ממני כלום מיד אמר הקב"ה המכסה אני מאברהם ונמלך בתורה ואמר לה בתי בואי ונשיאך לאברהם אהובי, אמרה לפניו לא עד שיבוא ענו ויצא ענוה מיד נמלך הקב"ה בספר יצירה ואמר כן ומסרו לאברהם והיה יושב יחיד ומעיין בו ולא היה יכול להבין בו כלום עד שיצאה בת קול ואמרה לו כלום אתה מבקש להשוות עצמך אלי אני אחד ובראתי בספר יצירה וחקרתי בו ואתה לא תוכל להבין בו יחיד קרב לעצמך חבר והביטו בו שניכם ותבינו בו מיד הלך אברהם לשם רבו וישב עמו ג' שנים והביטו וידעו לצור את העולם ועד עכשיו אין לך אדם שיבין בו יחיד אלא שני חכמים ולא יבינוהו עד ג' שנים ובשיבינוהו

[48]) Peter Beer, Geschichte religiöser Sekten der Juden, Zweiter Band, Brünn 1823, p. 10, 12. 21.

יכלו לעשות כל מהלבב [מה שלבם?] חפץ וכשהבין בו אברהם הוסיף
חכמה יתירה ולימד כל התורה כולה.

We find in an ancient reading as follows:

"When Abraham. our father was born, the angels of ministry said to the Holy One, Blessed be He: 'o Lord of the World! Thou hast a beloved one in the world, wilt thou conceal anything from him?' Directly, the Holy On blessed be He said, 'Shall I conceal from Abraham?' and consulted the Torah. He said to her, 'My daughter, come and we will marry thee to Abraham My beloved.' She said to him, 'No, not until the meek one comes and takes meekness.' God then consulted the Sefer Yetzirah, which said, 'Yes'. God then handed it over to Abraham, who sat by himself studying it, without being able to understand anything, until a heavenly voice came forth and said, 'Dost thou seek to compare thyself with Me? I am One I created the Sefer Yetzirah, and studied it. But thou canst not understand it alone. Get thee an associate, and look into it together, you will then understand.' At once, Abraham went to his teacher Shem, and stayed wit him three years. They looked into it and they knew how to form the world. From that time to this, there is no man who can understand it alone, there must be two wise men, and they cannot understand it before three years. But when they do understand it, they can do anything their hearts desire. When Abraham understood it, his wisdom increased greatly, and he taught the whole law."

The world which Abraham and his teacher Shem were able to form after three years of study of the Sefer Yetzirah may be understood to mean the world of letters. Indeed, the invention of letters was anciently spoken of as the creation of the universe.

The names of Moses, Ezra[49]), and Rabbi Akiba have also been advanced as the authors of the Sefer Yetzirah. The attribution of the work to Rabbi Akiba undoubtedly rests on a confusion of titles. The Sefer Yetzirah was called by ancient writers אותיות של אברהם אבינו, and was confounded with the Midrash אותיות של רבי עקיבא, which is called by some authors Sefer Yetzirah. Thus Gedaliah Ibn Yahya, in his „Shalshelet ha-Kabbalah, says :

והוא חבר ספר מכילתין וספר יצירה על הקבלה ויש ספר יצירה שחבר אברהם אשר הרמב"ן חבר פירוש גדול ונפלא עליו.

"He composed the Sefer Mechiltin, and the Sefer Yetzirah on Kabbalah. There is a Sefer Yetzirah composed by Abraham, to which Nachmanides made a great and wonderful commentary."

This passage was apparently misunderstood by some later writers, who imagined that Rabbi Akiba was the author of the Sefer Yetzirah attributed to Abraham. Hence Isaac de Lates; criticism in the introduction to the Zohar:

ועוד מי התיר לרבי עקיבא לכתוב ספר יצירה וקראוהו משנה שהיתה שומה בפיהם בקבלה מאברהם.

"Besides, who permitted Rabbi Akiba to write the Sefer Yetzirah? They called it Mishnah, and it was handed down to them by oral tradition from Abraham."

49) Peter Beer, Geschichte religiöser Sekten der Juden, zweiter Band, Brünn 1823, p. 12, 21.

Moses Gordovero[50] flatly denies Rabbi Akiba's authorship of the Sefer Yetzirah. In the Pardes Rimmonim he says:

והנה אתנו ספר יצירה המיוחס לאברהם אבינו עליו השלום ויש מיחסים אותו לרבי עקיבא ואינה מוסכמת.

"We have a Sefer Yetzira attributed to Abraham. Some ascribe it to Rabbi Akiba, but there is no general agreement."

Modern writers are also divided in their opinions concerning the age of the Sefer Yetzirah. Some of them believe it to be a production of the first or the second century B. C.; others place it in the Geonic period, ranging from the seventh to the ninth centuries of the Christian Era. My personal inclination is to accept the late date (about 750—931) for that portion of the book which has been referred to as Sefer Yetzirah II, in the discussion of the text: but I have no doubt that the part containing the account of the origin of letters, which was explained above is pre-Talmudic, and is reffered to in the Talmud in the following passages:

רבא ברא גברא (רש"י על ידי ספר יצירה שלמדו צרופי אותיות של שם) שדריה לקמיה דרבי זירא הוי קא משתעי בהדי ולא הוה קא מהדר ליה א"ל מן חבריא את הדר לעפרך. רב חנינא ורב אושעיה הוו יתבי כל מעלי שבתא ועסקי בספר יצירה ומיברי להו עיגלא תילתא ואכלי ליה[51].

כדרב חנינא ורב אושעיא כל מעלי שבתא הוו עסקי בהלכות יצירה ומיברי להו עיגלא תילתא ואכלי ליה[52].

50) Quoted from פרדס רמונים by L. Goldschmidt, Sefer Yetzirah Frankf., 1903.

51) Sanhedrin, 65 b.

52) Ibid, 67 b.

Raba created a man (Rashi says, through the Sefer Yetzirah), and sent him to Rabbi Zera who spoke to him, but received no answer. He then said to him, "you are a creature of the learned, return to your dust."

Rabbi Hanina and Rabbi Oshaiah sat the entire eve of the Sabbath studying the Sefer Yetzirah and created a three-year old calf, and ate it" . . . "Like the case of Rabbi Hanina and Rabbi Oshaiah who studied the Hilchot Yetzirah every Friday, and a three-year-old calf was created for them, which they ate".

The Sefer Yetzirah and the Hilchot Yetzirah, mentioned in these passages are undoubtedly our original Sefer Yetzirah, from which was borrowed the Baraitha beginning with the words of the Sefer Yetzirah:

תהו זה קו ירוק שמקיף את כל העולם כולו [53]

„Void is a green line that surrounds the whole universe."

This passage must have been a part of the original Sefer Yetzirah and not a later interpolation, for it tallies with the paragraphs before and after it, that its omission leaves a gap that no other can fill so satisfactorily

From a passage of a commentary on the Sefer Yetzirah of the thirteenth century, which is still extant in manuscript. (Bodleian Library, Codex 1947), we can see that the commentator believed that the Sefer Yetzirah was written by Joseph ben Uziel, for he says:

זה לשון יוסף בן עוזיאל מפי ירמיה קבל רוח הבור זה רוח הקדש . . .
וחשב יוצר על מכונו

[53] Hagigah, 12a.

"These are the words of Joseph ben Uziel, who received them from Jeremiah: 'Voice, air. speech', this is the holy spirit . . . . and restore the creator to his abode."

As the commentator declares words in the Sefer Yetzirah to be the language of Joseph ben Uziel, he evidently believed that he wrote it.

In another passage the commentator says.

כך יוסף בן עוזיאל מפי ירמיה הנביא נגלה סוד בבבל . . . .

„So Joseph ben Uziel received from Jeremiah the Prophet. The secret was revealed in Babylonia."

By סוד is apparently meant the Sefer Yetzirah [54], which he believed to have been revealed and transmitted to Joseph ben Uziel by the prophet Jeremiah. From the ending of this commentary we gather that the commentator had before him an ancient text of the Sefer Yetzirah, which had at the end סליק משנת אברהם ומשנת יוסף בן עוזיאל "Here ends the Mishnah of Abraham and the Mishnah of Joseph ben Uziel." Recanati and other writers took this colophon to mean that Joseph ben Uziel was the author of the commentary. This misunderstanding caused the bibliopraphers to catalogue it under the title ברייתא דיוסף בן עוזיאל or ספר יצירה.

In the Leipzig Codex (No. XXX, fol. 12) there is another treatise called ברייתא דיוסף בן עוזיאל, which A. Epstein [55]) considers a work by the same author as the commentary. The quoted title was given to the treatise apparently because of the following passage occurring therein:

תני יוסף בן עוזיאל שגילה לו ירמיה הנביא ואין לגלותו אלא לצנועים

[54]) Comp. Rashi on Jer. 23, 18 where סוד is explained by Sefer Yetzirah.

[55]) החוקר, Krakau-Wien 1893—95, II, p. 41.

"Joseph ben Uziel taught it. It was revealed to him by Jeremiah the prophet, and it must not be revealed to anyone except the pious" (the modest?). In this passage the author doubtless refers again to the Sefer Yetzirah, which was revealed or handed down by the prophet Jeremiah to Joseph ben Uziel.

J. J. L. Barges[56]) quotes, from the Paris Cod. 762 the following passage, which occurs also in the Brit. Mus. Cod. 15299 :

אלו הם ה׳ ספרים וה׳ סדרים שגלה בן סירא לעזיאל בנו וליוסף נכדו ספר יצירה ספר תגי [תגין] ספר דקדוק ספר פסיקתא רבתי בתרי אפי ספר זרובבל ויש בו ה׳ פרקים פרק ר׳ שמעון בן יוחי פרק אבות דרבי נתן פרק אותיות דר׳ עקיבא פרק מעשה משכן פרק דרך ארץ. ד׳ סדרים סדר עולם סדר פקודות סדר שעות סדר עבור סדר הלכות וכשגלה כל הדוים האלה רעשו כל צבא מרום ויצאה רוח הקדש אמרה מי הוא שגלה סתרי לבני אדם עמד עצט״ש [בן סירא] ואמר אני בוזי בן בוזי אמר לו דייך מיד ישב יוסף וכתב מפי עצט״ש [בן סירא] אלו הדברים וכתבן ה׳ ספרים בא״ין ספר יצירה וכו׳ . . . .

"These are the five Sefarim (books) and the five Sedarim (orders) which Ben Sira revealed to his son Uziel, and his grandson Joseph, Sefer Yetzirah, Sefer Tagin, Sefer Dikduk, Sefer Pesikta Rabbati in two forms, Sefer Zerubbabel, which contains five chapters: Simeon ben Yoḥai, Aboth di Rabbi Nathan, Otiot di Rabbi Aḳiba, Maase Mishkan, Derek Eretz. The five Sedarim are: Seder Olam, Seder Pekudoth, Seder Shaot, Seder Ibbur, Seder Halakoth. When he revealed all these secrets, all the host of heaven shook, and the holy spirit came out and said: 'Who is it that revealed my secrets to mankind? עצט״ש [Ben Sira] arose and said: 'I Buzi son of Buzi'. The holy

56) ספר תגין, Paris 1866, p. X.

spirit said to him: 'Enough'. Immediately Joseph sat down and wrote down these words at the dictation of עצמ"ש [Ben Sira], and he wrote them in five books on the earth: Sefer Yetzirah, etc."

Although the greater part of this passage is obviously spurious, attributing, as it does, to Joseph ben Uziel works of other authors, it may be authentic with regard to the Sefer Yetzirah, which heads the list. It is not unlikely that originally only the Sefer Yetzirah had been ascribed to Joseph ben Uziel, but as there were several other works in the same volume, some careless copyist attributed them all to him. The original passage may have read as follows:

זה הוא ספר יצירה שגלה בן סירא לעוזיאל בנו וליוסף נכדו וכשגלה הרז הזה רעשו כל צבא מרום ויצאה רוח הקדש אמרה מי הוא זה שגלה סודי לבני אדם עמד עצמ"ש ואמר אני בוזי בן בוזי, אמר לו דייך, מיד ישב יוסף וכתב מפי עצמ"ש ספר יצירה.

"This is the Sefer Yetzirah, which Ben Sira revealed to his son Uziel, and his grandson Joseph. When he had revealed this secret, all the hosts of heaven trembled, and the holy spirit came out and said: Who is it that has revealed my secret, to mankind? עצמ"ש arose and said: 'I Buzi son of Buzi'. Then the holy spirit said to him: 'Enough'. Immediately Joseph sat down and wrote down the sefer Yetzirah at the dictation of עצמ"ש."

This passage also indicates that Joseph ben Uziel wrote the Sefer Yetzirah. According to this passage, however, not Jeremiah but Ben Sira revealed the philosophy of the Sefer Yetzirah to his grandson Joseph ben Uziel. In the Alphabet of Ben Sira Josef ben Uziel is also mentioned as a grandson of Ben Sira and Ben Sira's mother was a daughter [57]) of Jeremiah. There are also legends that Jeremiah and his grandson Ben Sira studied together the Sefer Yetzirah.

The "ילקוט ראובני" 20a, Lemberg 1860, quotes from a cabalistic work פליאה, as follows:

ירמיה התחיל לעסוק בספר יצירה יצאה בת קול ואמרה קנה לך חבר, הלך אצל סירא בנו נתעסקו בספר יצירה בשנים . . . . ולבסוף שעשו הכלל והמאמר נברא להם אדם אחד והיה כתוב במצחו אמת והיה סכין בידי איתו הנברא והיה מוחק את א׳ של אמת א״ל ירמיהו מאי האי א״ל אמשול לך משל למה״ד לאחד שהיה בונה כמה בתים כמה מדינות כמה מגדלות ולא היה אדם מרגיש באומנתו ולא במלאכתו כלל עד שפיתוהו ב׳ בני אדם ולימדם סוד אומנתו עד שידעו הכל ע״ד האמת וכשידעו האומנו׳ וסודו ותכונתו התחילו לקנטרו בדברים עד שנפרשו בחכמתו ונעשים בנאים כמותו מה שהוא היה עושה בדינר הם עושים בג׳ פשוטים, וכשהרגישו בהם בני אדם הניחו כבודו שלוה האומן והולכים כולם אליהם ומכבדים אותם ועוסקים בהם בענין הבנין שהיו צריכי׳.

"Jeremiah began to study Sefer Yetzira, when a heavenly voice came forth and said: 'Get thee an associate'. He accordingly went to his son Sira, and they studied the Sefer Yetzira together. Finally . . . a man was created by them, upon whose forehead was written 'Emet' (אמת = truth). The person created had a knife in his hand, and was erasing the letter Aleph of the word Emet. Jeremiah said to him, 'Why do you that?'. He answered, 'I will tell you a parable'. This case is similar to that of a man who built many houses, countries, and towers, and no one appreciated his art or his work, until two men induced him to teach them the secret of his art, so that they knew it all thoroughly. When they learned the art, and the

[57]) See "Alphabet of Ben Sira", ed. Steinschneider Berlin 1858. 16b.

man's secret and method, they began to irritate him with their words, and finally left him, taking his science with them and became builders like him. What he did for a *denarius*, they did for three *peshutim*. When people learned of their existence, they all left the original artisan and went to them, honoring them, and negotiating with them in their building enterprises"

This passage, which may also be considered as having been prefixed originally to a copy of the Sefer Yetzira, not only indicates that Jeremiah and Ben Sira studied the philosophy of the Sefer Yetzira (or the invention of the alphabet), but also gives a reason why this study should be kept secret.

In his work *Sefer ha-Gematria*, Rabbi Judah he-Hasid says[58]):

בן סירא רצה לעסוק בספר יצירה יצאה בת קול ואמרה לא תוכל לעשותו לבדך הלך לו אצל ירמיהו אביו . . . ועסקו בו ולמקצה ג' שנים נברא להם אדם אחד וכתוב במצחו אמת כמו במצח אדם הראשון אמר להם האחד שבראו . . . הקב"ה . . . כשרצה להמית את אדם הראשון מחה אות מאמת ונמצא מת, כל שכן שאני רוצה לעשות כן ולא תבראו עוד אדם שלא יטעו בו העולם כדור אנוש. אמר להם אדם הנברא הפכו צרוף האותיות למפרע ומחקו א' מאמת שבמצחו ומיד נעשה לעפר.

"Ben Sira wanted to study the Sefer Yetzira, when a heavenly voice came out and said: 'Thou canst not do it alone'. So he went to his father Jeremiah . . . and they studied it. At the end of three years a man was created by them, on whose forehead was written Emet (אמת = truth), as on the forehead of Adam. Then the one whom they had created said to them: 'God created Adam, and when He wanted to put him to death, he erased a letter from the word Emet and it became Met

[58]) Quoted by Epstein in מקדמוניות היהודים, Wien 1887, p 122.

(מת = dead). So much the more reason is there why I should want to do the same, so that you may not again create a man and the world go astray through him like the generation of Enosh . .' Then the man who had been created said to them: 'Transpose the order of the letters, and erase the Aleph from the word Emet (אמת) in my forehead. Immediately he turned into dust."

A work like the Sefer Yetzirah could not have been the product of the person, who actually put it into writing. Its contents must have been known, to at least a few persons, long before it was written down. It is, therefore, not at all impossible that the prophet Jeremiah and his grandson Ben Sira studied its philosophy.

From the foregoing it is evident that so far we have no historic document by which to prove either the authorship or the exact age of the Sefer Yetzirah. According to the above quoted legendary passages, however, the Sefer Yetzirah was written by a Joseph ben Uziel, a grandson of Ben Sira. If this Ben Sira was the author of Ecclesiasticus, which apparently was written in the third century B. C. E., his grandson Joseph ben Uziel could have written the Sefer Yetzirah in the second century B. C. E. If, however, this Ben Sira was identical with the high-priest Joshua son of Jehozadak, his grandson Joseph ben Uziel could not have written the Sefer Yetzirah later than at the end of the fifth century B. C. E. The authors of the above quoted passages and the author of the Alphabet of Ben Sira doubtless believed Ben Sira to be identical with the high-priest Joshua son of Jehozadak, to whom the wisdom taugh in Ecclesiasticus was attributed.

Isidore of Sevile in his remote day (620), identified Jesus, the son of Sira, with Joshua ben Jehozadak, and in the Latin Mss. of Ecclesiasticus, it is stated that Ben Sira was a son of Jehozadak[59]). Like Ecclesiasticus, the Pseudo-Ben Sira's "Alphabet of ben Sira" was also attributed to Joshua ben Jehozadak. Hence its title in the Hebrew-German edition (Offenbach, 1728).

Already Abraham Abulafia perceived that the Pythagorean number philosophy is identical with the Sefiroth philosophy of the Sefer Yetzirah. The relation they bear to each other is variously explained. A. F. Thimus[60]), shares the view that the Pythagorean philosophy is an adaptation from the Sefer Yetzirah. Others hold that the author of the Sefer Yetzirah borrowed his philosophy from Pythagoras and Plato.

I do not pretend to be able to solve this difficult question. But I wish to call attention to a few points which may suggest a solution or at least guide further investigation.

The person of Pythagoras[61]) is as much an unknown quantity as that of Ben Sira. Philolaus, the first one to publish

[59]) See Nestle in Hasting's *Bible Dictionary*, vol IV, p. 542.

[60]) *Die Harmonikale Symbolik*, Köln 1876, II, pp. VI, 2, 133, 241.

[61]) Dr. A. Hirsh (*JQR.*, vol. XX, p. 61) doubts whether there ever was a Pythagoras, although he has no doubt there existed a Pythagorean school of philosophers. It is admitted (J. Burnet, *Early Greek Philosophy*, page 99) that "all that has come down to us under the names of various disciples of Pythagoras is pure forgery, of the most worthless kind. The whole early history of Pythagoreanism is therefore conjectural, and all we really know of the school is what we are told by Aristotle". According to some writers Pythagoras was a Greek, according to others, he was either a Phœnician or a Syrian. There have been also some writers

the Pythagorean philosophy, corresponds curiously to Joseph ben Uziel who wrote down the Sefer Yetzirah. Would it be to bold to conclude that the Sefer Yetzirah represents the genuine fragments of Philolaus?

ספר יצירה

(פרק א)

משנה א'

שלשים ושתים נתיבות פליאות חקק יה יהוה צבאות בסופר וספור וספר:

משנה ב'

אלו הן שלשים ושתים נתיבות פליאות עשר כפולות ושתים עשרה פשוטות שהן עשרים ושתים אותיות של תורה:

משנה ג'

עשר אותיות כפולות א, ב, ג, ד, ג, כ, פ, ר, ש, ת, עשר ולא תשע עשר ולא אחת עשרה. שתים עשרה אותיות פשוטות ה, ו, ח, ט, י, ל, מ, נ, ס, ע, צ, ק, שתים עשרה ולא אחת עשרה שתים עשרה ולא שלש עשרה

SEFER YETZIRAH

Chap. I

§ 1

Thirty-two mysterious ways has the Lord, Lord of hosts, ordained through Scribe, Script, and Scroll.

§ 2

These are the thirty-two mysterious ways, ten double and twelve simple, which are the twenty-two letters, of the Torah.

§ 3

The ten double letters are א, ב, ג, ד, ג, כ, פ, ר, ש, ת, ten and not nine, ten and not eleven. The twelve simple letters are ה, ו, ח, ט, י, ל, מ, נ, ס, ע, צ, ק, twelve and not eleven:

who believe that he was a Jew. (Rathgeber. *Grossgriechenland und Pythagoras*, Gotha 1866, pp. 325, 461, 466). He has even been identified with the prophet Ezekiel. (*Ibid*. 534). If Pythagoras was a Hebrew he should rather be identified with the high-priest Joshua son of Johozadak.

בחון בהן וחקור בהן והעמד דבר על בוריו והשב יוצר על מכונו:

twelve and not thirteen. Investigate them, examine them, establish the matter clearly, and restore the Creator to His abode.

משנה ד'

עשרים ושתים אותיות חקוקות בקול חצובות ברוח קבועות בפה בחמשה מקומות:

§ 4

Twenty-two letters are engraved by the voice, hewn out in the air, and fixed in the mouth in five places.

משנה ה'

עשרים ושתים אותיות חקקן חצבן שקלן והמירן צרפן וצר מהן את כל היצור ואת כל העתיד לצור:

§ 5

Twenty-two letters He engraved, hewed out, weighed, changed, combined, and formed out of them all existing forms, and all forms that may in the future be called into existence.

משנה ו'

כיצד צרפן שקלן והמירן? אלף עם כולן וכולן עם אלף, בית עם כולן וכולן עם בית, וכן כולן עם כולן חוזרות חלילה נמצא כל הדבור וכל היצור יוצא מהן:

§ 6

How did He combine them, weigh them, and change them? א with all of them and all of them with א; ב, with all of them and all of them with ב; and so all of them with all of them turning around in order; thus all words and all existing forms are derived from them.

משנה ו'

עשרים ושתים אותיות קבועות בגלגל בארבע מאות ושמונים וארבעה שערים ותוור הגלגל פנים ואחור וסימן לדבר עין למעלה ענג ועין למטה נגע:

§ 7

Twenty-two letters are fixed in a circle, with 484 divisions, and the circle turns forward and backward; thus in ענג [delight], the ע is at the beginning; in נגע [plague], the ע is at the end.

משנה ח'

שתי אבנים בונות שני בתים, שלש אבנים בונות ששה בתים, ארבע אבנים בונות עשרים וארבעה בתים חמש אבנים בונות מאה ועשרים בתים, שש אבנים בונות שבע מאות ועשרים בתים, שבע אבנים בונות חמשת אלפים וארבעים בתים, מכאן ואילך צא וחשוב מה שאין הפה יכול לדבר ואין האוזן יכולה לשמוע,

§ 8

Out of two stones two houses are built, out of three stones six houses are built, out of four stones twenty-four houses are built, out of five stones one hundred and twenty houses are built, out of six stones seven hundred and twenty houses are built, out of seven stones five thousand and forty houses are built. Go and count further, what the mouth is unable to prouounce, and the ear is unable to hear.

(פרק ב)

משנה ט'

צורף וממיר ועושה את כל היצור ואת כל הדבור בשם אחד נמצא כל היצור וכל הדבור יוצא משם אחד:

Chap. II

§ 9

He combines and changes and makes all forms and all speech with the one

Name: thus all forms and all speech are derived from the one Name.

משנה י׳

שלש אמות אמש סוד גדול מופלא ומכוסה שמהן יוצאים רוח מים אש, אש למעלה ומים למטה ורוח מכריע בינתים, וסימן לדבר מ״ם דוממת שין שורקת ואלף מכריע בינתים:

§ 10

Three vowels אמש constitute a great secret, marvellous and hidden. From them go forth air, water, and fire. Fire above and water below, and air holding the balance between them: thus מ is mute, ש is hissing, and א holds the balance between them.

משנה י״א

שלש אמות אמ״ת סוד גדול מופלא ומכוסה ומהן יוצאים רוח מים עפר, ארבע אמות אמש״ת שהן חמשה אבות שמהן נולדו עשרים ושבעה תולדות:

§ 11

Three vowels אמ״ת constitute a great secret, marvellous and hidden. From them go forth air, water, and earth. Four vowels אמש״ת, which are five vowels, that gave birth to twenty-seven consonants.

משנה י״ב

חמשה אבות כל אחד לבדו עומד ועשרים ושבעה תולדות כולם אדוקים באבות, עשאן כמין מדינה וערכן כמין מלחמה, ואדון יחיד אל מלך נאמן מושל בכולן ממעון קדשו עד עדי עד:

§ 12

The five vowels stand each one by itself, but the twenty-seven consonants are all dependent on the vowels. He made them in the form of a state, and arranged them like an army in battle array. The only One Master, God, the faithful King, rules over them from His holy abode forever and ever.

משנה י"ג

המשה אבות ועשרים ושבעה תולדות אלו עשרים ושתים אותיות שיסד יה יהוה צבאות מעשר ספירות ובלימה:

§ 13

The five vowels and twenty-seven consonants, these are contained in the twenty-two letters which the Lord, Lord of hosts, established out of the ten digits and zero.

פרק ג

Chap. III

משנה י"ד

עשר ספירות ובלימה בלום פיך מלדבר ולבך מלהרהר ואם רץ לבך שוב למקום כי על דבר זה נכרת ברית:

§ 14

The ten digits and zero — close thy mouth from speaking and thy heart from thinking, and if thy heart should leap, let it come back to its place: for concerning this has the covenant been made.

משנה ט"ו

עשר ספירות ובלימה נעוץ סופן בתחלתן ותחלתן בסופן כשלהבת קשורה בגחלת הבן בחכמה וחכם בבינה שאדון יחיד ואין לו שני ולפני אחד מה אתה סופר:

§ 15

The ten digits and zero, their end is joined with their beginning, and their beginning with their end, as the flame is attached to the coal. Understand wisdom and be wise in understanding, that there is but one Master, and there is no second to Him, and before One, what countest thou?

משנה ט״ו

עשר ספירות ובלימה צפייתן כמראה הבזק ותכליתן אין להן סוף דברו בהן ברצוא ושוב ולמאמרו כסופה ירדפו ולפני כסאו הן משתחוות:

§ 16

The ten digits and zero, their appearance is like lightning; to their aim there is no limit. They go and come at His word, and at His command they pursue like the whirlwind, and kneel before His throne.

משנה י״ז

אלה הן העשר ספירות ובלימה שבהן חקק את עולמו אל חי העולמים ברוך ומבורך שמו:

§ 17

These are the ten digits and zero, with which the Eternally Living God, blessed be His name, ordained His world.

משנה י״ח

אחת חקק וחצב בה קול רוח ודבור וזה רוח הקדש:

§ 18

One—He graved and hewed out of it voice, air and speech, and this is the Holy Spirit.

משנה י״ט

שתים חקק וחצב בהן תהו ובהו, תהו זה קו ירוק שמקיף את כל העולם כולו, ובהו אלו אבנים מפולמות המשוקעות בתהום שמהן יוצאים מים:

§ 19

Two—He graved and hewed out of them void and chaos. Void is a green line that surrounds the whole universe, and chaos refers to viscous stones, sunk in the abyss, whence water comes forth.

משנה כ׳

שלש חקק וחצב בהן רפש וטיט עשאן כמין ערוגה הציבן כמין חומה סככן כמין מעזיבה ויצק עליהם שלג ונעשה עפר:

§ 20

Three—He graved and hewed out of them mud and clay. He arranged them like a garden bed. He set them up like a wall. He covered them like a pavement, and poured upon them snow, and the earth was formed.

משנה כ״א

ארבע חקק וחצב בהן כסא הכבוד ואופנים ושרפים וחיות הקדש ומלאכי השרת:

§ 21

Four—He graved and hewed out of them the throne of glory, the ophanim, the seraphim, the holy animals, and the ministering angels.

משנה כ״ב

יצר מתהו ממש ועשה אינו ישנו וחצב אבנים גדולות מאויר שאינו נתפש וסימן לדבר עשרים ושתים מנין ורוח אחד:

§ 22

He formed existence out of void, and made something out of nothing, and hewed large stones out of intangible air, thus twenty-two in number one in spirit.

משנה כ״ג

גם את זה לעומת זה עשה האלהים, טוב לעומת רע, ורע לעומת טוב, טוב מטוב, ורע מרע, הטוב מבחין את הרע, והרע מבחין את הטוב,

§ 23

Also God set the one over against the other, good against evil, and evil against good; good out of good, and evil

טובה שמורה לטובים ורעה שמורה לרעים:

out of evil; good testing evil, and evil testing good; good is stored away for the good, and evil is stored away for the evil.

משנה כ״ד

§ 24

וכיון שעמד אברהם אבינו והביט וראה וחקר והבין וחקק והצב וצרף וצר וחשב ועלתה בידו הבריאה אז נגלה עליו אדון הכל וכרת ברית לו ולזרעו עד עולם, כרת לו ברית בין עשר אצבעות ידיו והוא ברית הלשון וכרת לו ברית בין עשר אצבעות רגליו והוא ברית המילה וקשר עשרים ושתים אותיות התורה בלשונו וגלה לו את סודן משכן במים דלקן באש רעשן ברוח ונתבן לעשר כפולות ושתים עשרה פשוטות:

When Abraham our father arose, he looked and saw and investigated and observed and engraved and hewed and combined and formed and calculated, and his creation was successful. Then the Master of all revealed Himself to him, and made a covenant with him and with his seed forever. He made a covenant with him on the ten fingers of his hands, and this is the covenant of the tongue; and on the ten toes of his feet, and this is the covenant of circumcision; and tied the twenty-two letters of the Torah to his tongue and revealed to him their secret. He drew them through water; stormed them through air, kindled them in fire, and melted them into ten double and twelve simple letters.

CORRECTIONS.

P. 6 l. 16 For heard me expressing my views read: heard my views

P. 12 l. 25 For conèeptions read conceptions

P. 16 l. 15 For o' read o,

P. 25 l. 16 For ˥, ˩ read ┬, ┴

P. 31 l. 8 For ϒ ‹ read ⋎ ❮

P. 37 l. 11 For thre read three

P. 40 l. 17 For tetters read letters

P. 40 l. 21 For then read ten

P. 43 l. 14 For Barseloni read Barceloni

P. 44 l. 8 For On read One

P. 44 l. 20 For wit read with

The variants to the Sefer Yetzirah I, the text of Sefer Yetzirah II, texts Mantua I and Mantua II will be found in the Hebrew edition of this work which will appear shortly.

I have to acknowledge my indebtedness to Dr. H. Malter for reading the proof-sheets; and also to Dr. Israel Davidson for suggesting a few improvements.

A SOLUTION OF THE PYTHAGOREAN NUMBER PHILOSOPHY
SUPPLEMENT TO "THE ORIGIN OF LETTERS AND NUMERALS"

BY PHINEAS MORDELL.

Copyright 1922 by Phineas Mordell.

The real reason why the Pythagoreans considered numbers to be the elements and origin of everything was that they believed numeral symbols to have preceded all other forms of writing.[1] This is what they really meant when they said: "Numbers by nature are the first and prior to all things." (Aristotle's *Metaphysics*, Book 1, Chapter 5). The letters of the earliest alphabet having been numeral symbols, all words were originally made up of numeral symbols or numbers.

In the Hebrew language which also resembles the Phoenician language, (and it was anciently believed that Pythagoras himself was a Phoenician) both "words" and "things" are designated by the term דברים. Since "words" is the equivalent of "things" the Pythagoreans said that all things (i.e. words) had their origin and composition in numbers.

Now according to both the Sefer Yetzira and the Pythagoreans, the four elements, fire, air, water, earth, emanated from the first four numbers, 1, 11, 111, 1111.

For Iamblichus (*Life of Pythagoras*, transl. by Th. Taylor, London, 1815, p. 332) says: "The fourth tetractys is of the simple bodies, fire, air, water and earth, which have an analogy according to numbers. For what the monad was in the first tetractys, that fire is in this. But the duad is air, the triad is

[1] "The invention of Signs to represent numbers is doubtless much older than any form of writing" (Chambers Encyclopaedia, 1893, Vol. VII, p. 548). "Numeral characters, were first invented because they were first necessary to mankind." (Th. Astle—*The Origin and Progress of Writing*, London 1784).

water and the tetrad is earth."[2] In the Sefer Yetzira however, air is associated with the number one, water with the number two, earth with the number three and fire with the number four.[3] The real four elements of the Pythagoreans were also a series of strokes 1, 11, 111, 1111, amounting to ten which were originally numbers and letters.

The key to the complete identification of the philosophy of Pythagoras with that of the Sefer Yetzira as interpreted in this thesis is the Zero. According to the Sefer Yetzira as explained above בלימה means Zero. Was the Zero a secret known to the Pythagoreans? A solution to this question will be found in the Pythagorean dualism.

The "one" in the Pythagorean dualism is the Symbol, I. Contrary to the prevailing opinion, I believe that the Pythagoreans regarded the Zero, 0, as the second element which was called the infinite, indeterminate duality, infinite binary, etc. In a binary system of notation the Zero is the second Symbol. We know now that even the decimal system of notation originated from the two symbols the one, I, and the Zero, 0. This is in perfect harmony with the Pythagorean formula that all numbers originated from two elements, the limited (the one, 1,) and the unlimited (the Zero, 0). Therefore, all things according to the Pythagoreans originated from two elements One, 1, and the

---

[2] "Die Pythagoreer fuehrten daheralles auf die Zahl und nicht auf die mathematischen Figuren zurueck" (S. A. Byk. *Die Vorsokratische Philosophie* 1. Leipzig 1876, p. 116).

[3] It is the "central fire" (fiery angels the throne of glory) that is associated in the Sefer Yetzira (above p. 61 para. 21) with the number four or ten which the principle of place value makes a harmonious one (see below about harmony). The harmonious one (zusammengefuegtes Eins) was confounded with the plain one and thus fire came to be regarded as the Pythagorean first material element..

Zero, 0.[4] Since One, 1 is the finite, the Zero, 0 is the true infinite of the Pythagoreans. The One, 1 was considered the Good, for it represents that which exists, but the Zero, 0 was called the evil, for it represents non-existence.

The Pythagoreans could not have meant by infinite duality the number two, as many writers believe, for as the one is finite, so the number two and every other number must also be finite. Moreover, in a binary system of notation the symbol one, 1 itself becomes two just as in a decimal system of notation the symbol one, 1 itself, becomes ten.

Boeckh (*Philolaos*, pp. 53, 140, 148) made it clear that the Pythagorean infinity which is identical with infinite duality is not a number at all. See also A. Heinze, *Metaphyische Grundlehren*, Leipzig, p. 26.[5]

As Leibnitz has represented God's Creation of the Universe out of chaos or nothing, by means of two digits as symbols, so some Pythagoreans also interpreted the one as God and the second element the infinite binary (the Zero, 0) as the visible world. (Plutarch's *Morals* translated by W. W. Goodwin, vol. III, p. 109. Boston 1870).

"The Deity, it is thought by some, was distinguished by the Pythagoreans as absolute unity, from unity conceived." (*A*

---

[4] The Chinese Philosophers even actually said that the circle 0 and the line —— are the first elements from which all writing and everything originated. (Thimus *Harmonikale Symbolik* Koeln 1876, vol. 1, pp. 79–83).

By the "bounded line" and "unbounded line" from which according to the Pythagoreans everything originated (Diels H. *Die Fragmente der Vorsokratiker* p. 250) they surely meant the line and the circle the symbols for one and zero.

[5] After having written this supplement I found that Mr. S. Klyce (*Universe* 1921 para. 43 f) advances the view that zero and infinity are logically identical.

History of Greek Philosophy, Dr. E. Zeller, translated by S. F. Alleyne, London 1881, vol. 1. p. 398.)

Such a view was apparently that of the Sefer Yetzira (above p. 59 para. 15) "Understand wisdom and be wise in understanding, that there is but one Master, and there is no second to him." So in תיקוני זוהר it is said אנת הוא חד ולא בחושבן Thou art one which is different from the one that is counted. So Solomon Ibn Gebirol in כתר מלכות says: אתה אחד ולא כאחד הקנוי והמנוי Thou art one and not as the one that is created and counted.

George Boole in *The Laws of Thought*, London 1854, p. 48, also says: "The respective interpretations of the symbols 0 and 1 in the system of Logic are Nothing and Universe."

In ancient times various interpretations were given to the two symbols 1 and 0, as the Platonic antithesis of "being" and "non-being." (Boole, ibid, p. 414,) and Leucippus's "Plenum" and "vacuum," into which all existence was resolved (Boole, ibid, p. 413). The Philosophy and religion of Dualism apparently arose from an interpretation of the symbols one, 1 and zero, 0.

Various views prevailed about the origin of these two symbols. Some believed that the Zero. 0 preceded the One, 1. Perhaps the Chinese cosmogony is based on this view.[6] The author of the Sefer Yetzira and the Pythagoreans believed that the one preceded the zero. Therefore, the zero was second.

The view held by some Kabbalists that the nine Sefiroth or numerals (1-9) have emanated from infinity-אין סוף implies that the Zero 0, has preceded the One, 1. But according to the author of the Sefer Yetzira and the Pythagoreans even infinity

[6] "There was first of all a period when Nothing existed . . . Gradually Nothing took upon itself the form and limitation of Unity, represented by a point at the centre of a circle" (H. A. Giles, *A History of Chinese Literature*, New York, 1901, p. 3).

-אין סוף emanated from the One, 1.

After the invention of the symbols 11, 111, 1111, when the binary system of notation developed into a decimal, the zero was regarded as the fifth symbol and hence the fifth element. The five symbols or elements 1, 11, 111, 1111, 0, were supposed to symbolize the whole cosmos which was believed to be in harmony with a decimal system of notation expressible by these symbols.[7]

[7]"Die Weltkugel besteht aus fuenf Koerpern: dies sind innerhalb der Kugel Feuer, Wasser, Erde, Luft und ausserdem fuenftens das Gehaeuse der Kugel selbst." (Nestle, *Die Vorsokratiker.* Jena 1908, p. 162).

The four elements, air, water, earth and fire were also symbolized by ten dots . .. . arranged in a triangular form and the sphere of void encompassing them was symbolized by a circle. Hence the void and the universe were symbolized by

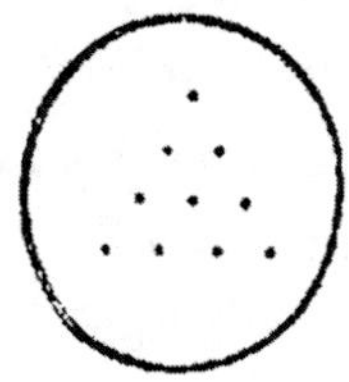

and apparently was simplified in a

which according to Boethius, the Neo-Pythagoreans used as a symbol for zero.

The void and the universe may also be symbolized by a circle containing the nine numeral figures 1–9. The nine numerals may be designated by Kabbalistic names as 1— חכמה, 2—בינה, 3—דעת, 4—חסד, 5—תפארת, 6—גבורה, 7—נצח, 8—דוד, 9—יסוד and the zero circle embracing them may be designated by אין סוף or כתר מלכות.

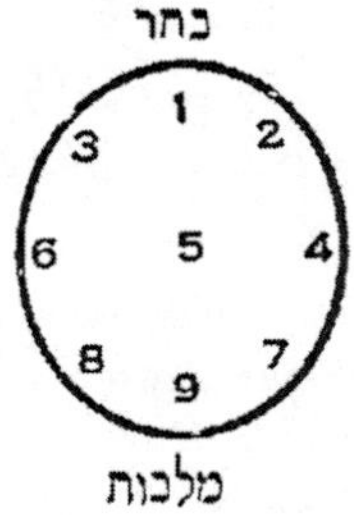

(About the Hebrew Kabbalistic origin of our numerals see A. J. H. Vincent in Journal de Mathematiques Par Joseph Liouville Paris 1839 pp. 261-280 and in Revue Archaelogique 1845-1846 pp. 601-621.)

According to the Sefer Yetzira the Hebrew alphabet consisting of ten double letters and twelve simple leters, representing the vigesimal and duodecimal systems of notation, still more fully symbolizes the universe.

If we consider every stroke as a separate symbol the zero is the eleventh as 1,1,1,1,1,1,1,1,1,1,0, or the tenth as 1,1,1,1,1,1,1,1,1,0

From a Pythagorean point of view the fifth element "aether" like infinity is only another name for vacuum.[8] Therefore, aether also is logically identical with zero (Com. above p. 30). Now "modern physics following Einstein asserts that . . . since the 'aether' as a substance obstinately evades all our attempts at observing it, and all phenomena occur as if it did not exist, the word 'aether' lacks physical meaning, and therefore aether does not exist" (M. Schlick, *Space and Time*, p. 12). "Since we are free to use words at pleasure there is no objection to using the word 'aether' in the future to represent the vacuum . . . we must be very cautious, however, not to picture it as matter" (ibid p. 20).

In the above explained system of notation from which our system of notation originated, the principle of position (place value) plays an important role. It is this principle that makes it possible to express all numbers, by only two symbols the One, 1 and the Zero, 0. The principle of position is the "miracle" that makes one, many and many, one. In the Sefer Yetzira (above p. 59 para. 15) the principle of position is indicated by the words "The ten digits and zero their end is joined with their beginning,

"[8]Das fuenfte Element ist also nicht aus der fuenften mathematischen Figur geworden, da dasselbe als Urgrund ganz formlos ist. Deswegen spricht auch Stobaeus von blos vier Elementen, . . . weil das fuenfte Element als reiner Urgrund noch keine Zahl und daher im Kosmos nicht voshanden ist." (S. A. Byk, *Die Vorsokratische Philosophie* I. Leipzig 1876, p. 94).

"Infinity is not the affirmation of space but its disappearance" (H. Waldon Carr, *The General Principles of Relativity* 1920, p. 152).

Perhaps it is more correct to read (above p. 60 para. 16) ותכליתן אין סוף "and their termination is infinity" instead of ותכליתן אין להן סוף "to their aim there is no limit."

as a flame is attached to the coal." Now if the Pythagorean number philosophy was based on such a system of notation as that on which the philosophy of the Sefer Yetzira is based, the principle of position, (place value) must have been known to the Pythagoreans and must have played an important role in their philosophy. But how did they express it? Did their "harmony" mean the principle of position?[9]

The Pythagorean philosophy is the greatest enigma of all philosophical systems of antiquity. Various sources such as Egyptian, Indian, Greek, Phoenician, Hebrew, etc., have been advanced as the origin of the Pythagorean philosophy. Many years of study have convinced me that the Pythagorean philosophy is identical with the philosophy of the Sefer Yetzira and both are of Hebrew origin. The philosophy of the Sefer Yetzira apparently emanated from the Hebrew prophetic guild or school as conjectured by Joseph Molitor. That which really was the philosophy of the Sefer Yetzira, the Greeks designated as Pythagorean philosophy and transmitted this to posterity in such a mutilated form that in spite of everything that has been written on the Pythagorean philosophy since Aristotle, it has never yet been really understood. The entire Greek account of Pythagoras and his philosophy is unreliable and most likely is a forgery. However, that may be, I hope I have at least succeeded in removing some obstacles to a better understanding of the Sefer Yetzira and the Pythagorean philosophy and their relation to each other.

---

[9] "Das absolute Princip dieser Harmonie sahen die Pythagoraeer in der Monas, sie ist ihnen die nur im Gedanken vorhandene mit sich selbst noch unentzweite Einheit, die das viele zu ihrem Gegensatze hat. In diesem Stadium ist sie nur Monas. Zur Harmonie wird sie erst, wenn sie aus sich selbst zum Vielen wird." (S. A. Byk, ibid, p. 108).